NATIVE AMERICAN PENTECOST
PRAXIS, CONTEXTUALIZATION, TRANSFORMATION

Native American Pentecost

Praxis, Contextualization, Transformation

Corky Alexander

Cherohala Press
Cleveland, Tennessee

Native American Pentecost
Praxis, Contextualization, Transformation

Published by Cherohala Press
900 Walker ST NE
Cleveland, TN 37311
USA
email: cptpress@pentecostaltheology.org
website: www.pentecostaltheology.org

Library of Congress Control Number: 2011940879

ISBN-10: 1935931245

ISBN-13: 9781935931249

DEDICATION

To my wife, Dr. Kimberly Ervin Alexander,
who more than any other individual embodies the example of
what a scholar should be. Her encouragement, love, and support
helped to sustain my commitment for the forgotten nations
of the world and this work that might bolster their cause.

Contents

ACKNOWLEDGEMENTS

I would like to express my deep appreciation to each one who helped make this work a reality. Without the assistance of my family and many dear pastors and scholars, my doctoral studies would not have been completed. Special thanks go to my mentor, R. Daniel Shaw and his wife Georgia, along with Drs. Betsy Glanville and Ryan Bolger. I would also like to thank Randy and Dr. Cheryl Bear-Barnetson, Dr. Richard Twiss, Larry 'Grizz' Brown, Kyle Taylor, Dan Lundy, J.R. Lilly, Jerry Tom, Ron Harvey, J.C. 'High Eagle' Elliot, Dr. Lee Roy Martin, Dr. Richard Waldrop, Fernando Ramirez, Judi Brodeen, and the Native Pentecostal churches in California, Oregon, and New Mexico for their open hearts and efforts to help facilitate the successful completion of the research which I conducted in Indian Country. I am very grateful to the Creator for each of the many faithful people whom he used to shape my life and guide my steps as I walked this road of faithful obedience. I appreciate the editors at CPT Press, John Christopher Thomas and Lee Roy Martin, for recognizing the value of my research and for their assistance in publishing it.

INTRODUCTION

E. Stanley Jones,[1] in speaking of the need for contextual and indigenous leadership in the nation of India, concluded his discussion of the mission of the church with these words:

> There is a beautiful Indian marriage custom that dimly illustrates our task in India, and where it ends. At the wedding ceremony the women friends of the bride accompany her with music to the home of the bridegroom. They usher her into the presence of the bridegroom – that is as far as they can go; then they retire and leave her with her husband. That is our joyous task in India: to know Him, to introduce Him, to retire – not necessarily geographically, but to trust India with the Christ and trust Christ with India. We can only go so far – He and India must go the rest of the way.[2]

As the body of Christ, expressed through denominational churches, nondenominational churches, and para-church organizations, struggles to overcome the mistakes of the past and take hold of future opportunities, the Lord of the Church proves himself faithful to call and empower that same Church to reach an end-time harvest. Pockets of unreached people groups still exist in portions of our world, awaiting the anointed witness of Christ's Church.

There is a group that remains largely unchurched, but not due to its remoteness to North America, as India does, or lack of historical orientation to Christianity. They have suffered a rather different

---

[1] E. Stanley Jones is an important figure in the topic of contextualization because of his 'Christian Ashrams'.

[2] E. Stanley Jones, *The Christ of the Indian Road* (New York: Abingdon Press, 1925), p. 71.

fate. They have been overreached, abused, and even massacred by armies led by organized church leaders. Their children have, in many cases, been stripped of their indigenous culture and imprisoned in boarding schools that, of necessity, required a cemetery installed for reasons that most individuals would shudder to learn. They are American Indians, First Nations people or Native Americans (to use a broader term). They are the host peoples of the North American continent, who rescued and cared for many of the early colonists, who in turn repaid their favors with infinitely less.[3] The American Indian church is a bride that has been and continues to be raped and bound by ignorance and prejudice.[4]

The Church still needs to repent of the genocide and, though not able to repair the breaches and wounds completely, must at least move to a position of respect and trust, answering the prayers of missionaries like E. Stanley Jones and Roland Allen.[5] It is now time for non-Natives to cease acting on behalf of Native Americans and encourage their honest attempts to discern their own spirituality and destiny.

There are, however, some positive developments taking place where Native believers are recovering their traditional practices and bringing about an integrated expression of their faith. My research trips to California, Oregon, South Dakota, Arizona, and Oklahoma have given me sights and words to describe the wonderful works of God among the sincere hearts of Native people as they are seeking to express fully their Indianness, worshiping in the power of the Holy Spirit. My heart has been strengthened and my life enriched as a result of the new relationships that have been the fruit of my journeys.

The topic of this study pertains to the missiological implications of traditional Native American practices in Pentecostal worship and church life. I intend to explain the significance that Native Americans are giving to traditional Native American practices in Pentecostal worship, and how members of the Native American Contextual Movement are integrating these practices. In light of the mis-

---

[3] Mark McDonald, 'The Gospel Comes to North America', *Journal of North American Institute for Indigenous Theological Studies* 4 (2006), p. 131.

[4] Vine Deloria, Jr., *God Is Red: A Native View of Religion* (Golden, CO: North American Press, 2nd edn, 1973), pp. 254-66.

[5] Roland Allen, *The Spontaneous Expansion of the Church and the Causes Which Hinder It* (Grand Rapids: Eerdmans, 1962).

sional difficulties between Euro-Americans and Native Americans, there is a need for constructive theological and missiological reflection to be done in considering the fruit realized in movements such as the American Indian Contextual Movement. There is a great gulf fixed between Native Americans who have become members of denominational churches and those, some of whom are traditionalists, who have not yet professed Christ and joined the Church. I am convinced that this work of critical reflection will serve as a respectful act of protocol, moving toward future forgiveness and reconciliation between Native and Euro-Americans as well as preparation for future missional progress in North America.

I am a Pentecostal church planter who, along with my family, was blessed to see two urban congregations birthed which included oppressed peoples. This is the source of my burden for this study. I have also been a pastor of established churches and have served as a denominational leader, and have a sense of the type of ignorance and prejudice that prevents outsiders from fully participating in the Christian community.

I have attempted in my research to identify Native American practices in the context of Pentecostal worship that will reduce syncretism while speaking to both Christian and non-Christian Native Americans. The goal of this is to enable the Native American Pentecostal community to proceed with an integrated Christian witness for a relevant approach to evangelism by using Native traditional practices conducive to Pentecostal worship.

It is my prayer that this study will contribute to the growth of Native ministries in the Church of God (Cleveland, TN), as well as other Pentecostal churches, and it is in this hope that I have delimited my study to Pentecostal churches. It is also my prayer that Native American concerns will be benefited in terms of missiological study. This work has been done at a time in which there are increasing missiological contributions of Native Americans at such places as Asbury Theological Seminary[6] in Kentucky, and at the time of the emergence of the North American Institute of Indige-

---

[6] See, for example, Richard Twiss, 'Native-led Contextualization Efforts in North America, 1989-2009' (DMiss, Asbury Theological Seminary, Wilmore, KY, 2010), and Randy Woodley, 'The Harmony Way: Integrating Indigenous Values within Native North American Theology and Mission' (PhD, Asbury Theological Seminary, Wilmore, KY, 2010).

nous Theological Studies. I desire to join this conversation as an act of celebration of these happy developments for Native Americans. I have intended that this study will help to identify traditional Native practices that can be contextualized in Native Pentecostal churches, and how these practices facilitate spiritual worship and witness.

Several questions are in order at this juncture:

1. What are historical examples of Natives using traditional practice in worship?
2. How do Native American traditional practices enhance Pentecostal worship?
3. In what way are traditional practices helpful in Pentecostal worship and witness?

For clarification, I would like to give several definitions that I will use in this study:

- Historical examples: Historical examples of how Native practices have or have not been included in Christian churches.
- Traditional practices: The music, dance, and related ceremonies peculiar to several Native American congregations will be described and how some of them have or have not been contextualized into Pentecostal worship.
- Pentecostal worship: The orality, music, dance, sacraments, healing practice, ecstasy, and prayer practices as expressed in the historic American Pentecostal Movement will be discussed and their conduciveness to Native American contextualization.
- Native American: I am using this as a broad term of all Native peoples of North America, including Canada.
- American Indian: I am using this term as a particular term that many Native Americans prefer, though never in reference to Natives of Canada.
- First Nations: This term would refer in particular to those host peoples of Canada, although all Native Americans could be included in the some 500 nations that existed at the time of first contact.

There are two foci that delimit this study: the large number of traditional practices and the variety of churches in the Native American context. The first delimitation pertains to the myriad of traditional practices through which these many peoples express their faith. These are far too numerous to engage in one study. Therefore, I have identified several practices that impact and serve to reflect on the nature of traditional practices in a church environment that others have not yet studied. As a result, I will delimit my study to practices that emphasize ceremonial activity.

With the interest of making a significant contribution to my denomination, I further delimit this study to Pentecostal churches by studying ceremonial activity in the following congregations:

- The Azusa Centennial Native American Gathering
- First Nations Foursquare Church, Santa Fe Springs, California
- Window Rock Church of God, Window Rock, Arizona
- Sacred Ground Outreach, Siletz, Oregon
- Eagle Butte Church of God, Eagle Butte, South Dakota
- Bacone College Chapel, Muskogee, Oklahoma
- Cherokee Church of God, Cherokee, North Carolina
- Living Way Foursquare Church, Apple Valley, California
- Ordination Service, East Ridge, Tennessee

In these contexts, Pentecostals are actively involved in utilizing traditional practices in order to ensure both their relevant Native American identification and their worship of the one true God.

I approach this project with some assumptions. Unlike some early and contemporary missionaries to Native Americans,[7] I am assuming that it is possible to recover traditional tribal practices and integrate them into Christian worship without harmful syncretistic results. I believe the Bible gives examples that can be used to support this conviction. Secondly, I assume that by using the word 'Pentecostal' I will communicate the nature of a historic movement that proceeded from the American Holiness Movement, flowered in the Azusa Street experience of 1906, and popularly characterized

---

[7] C.S. Smith, *Boundary Lines: The Issue of Christ, Indigenous Worship and Native American Culture* (Prince Albert, Sask.: N.C.E.M, 2001). *http://www.nativealliance. org/resources.htm.*

by the experience of speaking in tongues as the initial evidence of the baptism in the Holy Spirit. This heritage and theological positioning distinguishes my research from those working in non-Pentecostal environments.

I have organized the presentation of my research to reflect in Chapter 1 on the nature of the literature dealing with the status of Native American practices. I survey the important sources related to the topic of Native American worship patterns and engage the theories represented in them. Some of the sources emerge from mission history. These provide examples of the few times that missionaries encouraged Native traditional practices used in proximity of the Church. During this era, the guiding theories were civilization[8] and assimilation. I will recognize and honor a few cases where missionaries varied from the dominant approach. To accomplish this, I will address the development of the powwow movement and pan-Indianism as important sociological phenomena paving the way for inter-tribal ministry.

Also in Chapter 1, I trace the history of Native American ministries in the Church of God (Cleveland, Tennessee). This relates to the significance of the study, demonstrating that any recommendations for future change must respect and acknowledge the contributions of past leaders. Chapter 1 also traces the development of a pneumatological Pentecostal theology of religions, which is important for the study. Other sources are missiological in nature and address issues such as syncretism and critical contextualization. Happily, a few of these resources were actually written by Native Americans who are presently exploring the nature of their practices. Richard Twiss (Rosebud Lakota/Sioux) has set forth an engaging response to criticisms of the Contextual Movement, which serves as a Native voice on the subject of critical contextualization.[9] Prohibitions by groups such as The Christian and Missionary Alliance (CMA) offer an opportunity for me to discuss the use of sacred objects in Pentecostalism. Here I will show the ways in which Pen-

---

[8] The theory of civilization is based on the prejudicial belief that indigenous peoples were savages and that education could result in a more 'civilized' person, hence the term 'five civilized tribes' as a designation for the Cherokee, Chickasaw, Choctaw, Creek, and Seminole tribes.

[9] Richard Twiss, *Dancing Our Prayers: Perspectives on Syncretism, Critical Contextualization and Cultural Practices in First Nations Ministry* (Vancouver: Wiconi Press, 2002).

tecostalism makes room for Native American contextualization. I then outline the methods I employed in the study.

In Chapter 2, I give voice to Native Americans that are contextualizing traditional practices by utilizing participant observation, personal interviews, and case studies to examine the active contextualization that is taking place in several contexts.

In Chapter 3, I present several case studies from which I was able to gain a new appreciation of the ceremonial practices that are alive and well in Christian Native American spirituality and the impact of these practices on Christian worship. It is my intention in this chapter to detail the significant practices that are being utilized in my context, following a process of critical contextualization that is modified by a pneumatological, Pentecostal theology of religions and give a description of the transformed practices. These are the findings discovered in my observations of the worship services, as well as in the personal interviews. This follows the general order of history of the practice, data, critical contextualization, biblical literature, practice description, comparison, and finally, the transformed practice.

In Chapter 4, I discuss, through a process of theological reflection, the theory of contextualization and how it needs to be revised in order to serve the Native population. I further develop the internal model that is necessary to appreciate the discerning methods of a distinctly Native American contextualization.

In Chapter 5, I further discuss the related practices and show how implementing them in Pentecostal worship reduces syncretism and moves people closer to God. The relevance of these practices in a Pentecostal context is discovered through interaction between the literature and data.

In Chapter 6, I present some conclusions that lead me to make recommendations I hope will enable Native American Pentecostal believers to impact their non-Christian brothers and sisters in appreciating the relationship between ceremonial activity and the true worship of God. By 'true worship of God' I mean a worship that appropriately integrates, in a holistic way, the tradition and experience of Native peoples, as well as Scripture and reason. I will then lay out the trajectory I believe Pentecostal theology extends onto the subject, and what relevance it holds for my research.

This study has been the fruit of a personal journey that began in 2003. This journey has spiritual, familial, and geographic significance for me. It is my prayer that this study will contribute to the growth of Native ministries in the Church of God and other Pentecostal churches, and it is in this hope that I have delimited my study to Pentecostal churches. It is also my prayer that Native American concerns will be benefited in terms of missiological study done in conjunction with the recent and increasing missiological contributions of Native Americans.

PART ONE

DEVELOPING THE STUDY

1

DIVERSE VOICES:
LITERATURE REVIEW AND BACKGROUND

Billy Graham stated,

> In 1976 the United States celebrated its bicentennial as an inde-
> pendent government, but the ancestry of the Indian cannot be
> traced to the Mayflower or the American Revolution. They were
> here long before the Europeans arrived. The Indian is the origi-
> nal American. The Indian has been called 'the vanishing Ameri-
> can'. This is a misnomer. The Indian is the fastest growing eth-
> nic group in America. The Indian population of America is far
> greater than when Columbus arrived here from Spain, and those
> of mixed blood number in the millions. Today more than thirty
> thousand Indians are in universities and colleges and technical
> schools throughout the country. America now has hundreds of
> fine Indian doctors, engineers, educators, attorneys and clergy-
> men.[1]

In this chapter I survey the important sources related to Native
American use of spiritual practice and engage the theories represented in them. I begin with non-Native voices, then Native voices,
reviewing in each section history, anthropology, theology, and missiology.

---

[1] Cited in Tom Claus and Dale W. Kietzman (eds.), *Christian Leadership in Indian America* (Chicago: Moody Press, 1976), p. 48.

Non-Native Voices

In the light of the fact that until recent times most of the historical sources regarding Native Americans were authored by individuals outside the culture, it is necessary to consult non-Native works. I do this while at the same time remaining keenly aware that they are, for the most part, not written from the Native perspective.

Historical Literature

The historical literature consulted for this study began with those titles most familiar to scholars of American Indian studies. These include a number of references to the successes and failures of missionaries, and a few references to isolated instances of contextualization. In Pentecostal histories, it is possible to trace the story of Native missions in the various Pentecostal denominations. The first group serves my study as foundational and the second points to my significance as a Pentecostal scholar writing about Pentecostal Natives.

Non-Pentecostal Historical Literature

Non-Native Americans are puzzled about anything Native because of a worldview and ethos that is European in nature. Most of the histories of Native Americans and the American Indian wars that took place in this nation's history are essentially military histories, written from the victor's perspective.[2] Consequently, the close relationship between agencies such as the American Board of Commissioners for Foreign Missions and the United States Government skews the histories toward a non-Native perspective. To find accounts of Natives exercising self-determination in any religious or ceremonial way that is honored by Christian memory, it is necessary to consult newer histories written with the Native American perspective in mind.[3] There are a few bright spots.

---

[2] E.g. R.D. Edmunds, *American Indian Leaders: Studies in Diversity* (Lincoln, NE: University of Nebraska Press, 1980).

[3] E.g. C.S. Kidwell, *Choctaws and Missionaries in Mississippi, 1818-1918* (Norman, OK: University of Oklahoma Press, 1995); A.M. Josephy, *500 Nations: An Illustrated History of North American Indians* (New York: Alfred A. Knopf, 1994); J. Wilson, *The Earth Shall Weep: A History of Native America* (New York: Grove Press, 1998); W.G. McLoughlin, *Cherokees and Missionaries, 1789-1839* (Norman: University of Oklahoma Press, 1995).

William McLoughlin's 1995 history of the Cherokees' interactions with Protestant missionaries is such a volume. I have noticed that Natives quote this with respect. McLoughlin notes the conflict and interaction between the Baptist and Methodist methodologies and spiritualities, in which the spiritual practices of the Methodists seem to be more attractive to the Indians. This points in the direction of my own work, as John Wesley is the paternal grandfather of the Pentecostal Movement.

The civilization and assimilation approaches are described in most historical volumes as 'ideologies' as well as 'developing governmental policies'. Sadly, it was these policies that historically ravaged Indian populations and have continued to impact these peoples into contemporary times. These theories and their impact on European missionary endeavor are traced and critiqued in David Bosch's seminal work.[4]

Robert Berkhofer gives a sad conclusion to the choices that Indians had to make concerning Christian expression:

> Thus the advance of Indian Christianity was both hailed and depreciated. Even so simple a thing as whether the observer preferred a religion stressing strong doctrinal knowledge or more emphasis upon emotional fervor determined the outcome of the analysis, for it was easier for the Indians to display the latter than the former. Or the more exclusive a religion the observer considered Christianity, the more he searched for and condemned syncretistic practices, and the fewer Christians he could find.[5]

A trilogy of works that has developed into a theological tradition for American Indians are those by John G. Neihardt[6] and Joseph Epes Brown.[7] This material is important in that it is a narrative theology of Native Americans that has been used as a sort of 'bible'

---

[4] David J. Bosch, *Transforming Mission: Paradigm Shifts in Theology of Mission* (Maryknoll, NY: Orbis Books, 1991).

[5] R.F. Berkhofer, *Salvation and the Savage: An Analysis of Protestant Missions and American Indian Response, 1787-1862* (Lexington: University of Kentucky Press, 1965), p. 157.

[6] J.G. Neihardt, *Black Elk Speaks* (Lincoln: Bison Books, 2004), p. xiii; John Neihardt, *When the Tree Flowered: The Story of Eagle Voice, a Sioux Indian* (Lincoln, NE: University of Nebraska Press, new edn, 1991).

[7] Joseph Epes Brown, *The Sacred Pipe: Black Elk's Account of the Seven Rites of the Oglala Sioux* (Civilization of the American Indian Series; Norman, OK: University of Oklahoma Press, 1989).

for Indian religion. Also of importance is that Nicholas Black Elk was a Roman Catholic lay preacher and shaman. His work represents a contextualized Native Christian healing tradition.[8] Similarly, James Mooney's Cherokee work offers the record of a Cherokee shaman, Swimmer, who was also a Baptist preacher.[9] These describe an early period when Natives were practicing tribal traditional religion and Christianity at the same time.

The significance of these works is that they clearly represent a dualistic practice of traditional and Christian practices, which many Indians still utilize today. A history written by a non-Native, but highly respected by the Native American world, is Alvin Josephy's history.[10] Though written on a more popular level and serving primarily as an accompaniment book for Kevin Costner's documentary (1995/2004) of the same name (*500 Nations*), Josephy's work describes with sensitivity the painful history and destruction of cultures. One would think that Native beliefs would be wiped out completely by the hard work of Euro-Americans!

> We might suppose that the advent of Christianity upon the continent and the subsequent missionary expeditions that traversed the country have altered the religious traditions of the people beyond recall. In fact, generally speaking, this was the intent of Christianizing movements, since they judged Indian religious beliefs and practices as pagan and hostile to the spread of the faith they preached.[11]

Though Native peoples still exist, a certain degree of assimilation has taken place. It has not, however, taken place to the extent to which their oppressors had hoped or even thought, as Native Americans are able to integrate creatively those cultural dimensions that they feel are helpful, as well as live life on at least two planes: Indian and Christian. The anthropological and missiological material will speak to this subject more directly.

---

[8] A. Porterfield, *Healing in the History of Christianity* (New York: Oxford University Press, 2005), pp. 130-32.

[9] James Mooney, *Myths of the Cherokee: Nineteenth Annual Report of the Bureau of American Ethnology to the Secretary of the Smithsonian Institution 1897-1898 by J.W. Powell Director, in Two Parts* (St. Clair Shores: Scholarly Press, 1970/1990).

[10] Josephy, *500 Nations*.

[11] K.M. Dugan, *The Vision Quest of the Plains Indians: Its Spiritual Significance* (Lewiston, NY: Edwin Mellen Press, 1985), pp. 5-6.

Pentecostal History

The Pentecostal movement has spread among Native Americans as it has around the world. An important work I consulted for this study, *The New International Dictionary of Pentecostal and Charismatic Movements*, includes an article on Native American Pentecostals by David J. Moore.[12] Moore was influential in my going to Fuller Seminary and choosing this topic. Unfortunately, the scope of the article is limited to Southwestern tribes.

Cecil M. Robeck, Jr.'s recent history of the Azusa Street Revival, Charles Conn's history of the Church of God, Paul H. Walker's autobiography, J.J. Saggio and Jim Dempsey's historical description of the American Indian College, Darrin J. Rodgers' history of Pentecostalism in North Dakota, and Angela Tarango's recent dissertation are helpful.[13] However, none of these histories refers to any degree of contextualization (other than language) among Pentecostals. That which *is* relevant for my study are the histories of missions of the Church of God (Cleveland, TN) among Native Americans. In discussing the historical events surrounding the Church of God (Cleveland, TN), I hope to orient the reader to the developments that brought this historic Pentecostal denomination to this point in its outreach to Native Americans.

The Azusa Street Revival
Native people have been part of the Pentecostal movement from its inception, and Native Americans fully participated.[14] Robeck recounts stories of people of various cultures worshiping together. One story tells of a miraculous healing at the mission, where an in-

---

[12] S.M. Burgess and E.M. Van der Maas (eds.), *The New International Dictionary of Pentecostal and Charismatic Movements* (Grand Rapids: Zondervan Pub. House, 2002), pp. 926-27.

[13] Cecil M. Robeck, Jr., *The Azusa Street Mission and Revival: The Birth of the Global Pentecostal Movement* (Nashville: Thomas Nelson, 2006); Charles W. Conn, *Like a Mighty Army: A History of the Church of God Definitive Edition* (Cleveland: Pathway Press, 1994); Paul H. Walker, *Paths of a Pioneer* (Cleveland, TN: Pathway Press, 1970); J.J. Saggio and Jim Dempsey, *American Indian College: A Witness to the Tribes* (Springfield, MO: Gospel Publishing House, 2008); D.J. Rodgers, *Northern Harvest: Pentecostalism in North Dakota* (Bismarck, ND: North Dakota District Council of the Assemblies of God, 2003); Angela Tarango, "'Choosing the Jesus Way:' the Assemblies of God's Home Missions to American Indians and the Development of a Pentecostal Indian Identity' (PhD diss., Duke University, 2009).

[14] Robeck, *The Azusa Street Mission and Revival*, pp. 88, 142, 237.

digenous woman prayed the prayer of faith; the testimony of her healing was published in *The Apostolic Faith* magazine.[15] According to Robeck, early Pentecostals believed that one of the miraculous tongues spoken was Chippewa. Native Americans were present and fully participating in the Azusa Street revival, putting their mark on the Global Pentecostal Movement.

Golden Valley, North Dakota

With Native Americans clearly active at Azusa Street, it was not surprising to see that the first seeds of American Indian mission work in the Church of God have Azusa St. connections. Many of the early developments in this organization, as with most Pentecostal groups, can be traced to the Los Angeles outpouring. The mission work began in the Northwest when Maud and Lula Bishop of Thunder Hawk, South Dakota, received the baptism of the Holy Ghost in W.J. Seymour's Zion City, Illinois, meeting. About the same time that they returned home, Jasper B. Matthews, who had received the baptism of the Spirit at the Azusa Street Mission, felt called to go to Golden Valley, North Dakota. He felt he should go there and pray for a woman who was nearing death. The woman was Josephine Walker, and she was indeed healed in response to the preacher's prayer.[16]

The first Church of God in the Northwest was established in Josephine and E.M. Walker's house. J.W. Barker, the appointed pastor, later set in order a second church. According to Indians who were present, the pastor, Robert Merrifield, was said to have spoken the Mandan language when he was Spirit baptized. Merrifield had a strong burden for Native Americans. E.M. and Josephine Walker, along with their son, Paul H. Walker and his wife Margaret, had a great ministry, opening their home to Native people.[17]

---

[15] It is told that Father Juan Crespi named the place 'Azusa', an old Indian word that means 'blessed miracle', after a notable miracle resulted from a young Native girl's prayer.

[16] Conn, *Like a Mighty Army: A History of the Church of God Definitive Edition*, p. 155.

[17] Charles W. Conn, *Like a Mighty Army: A History of the Church of God* (Cleveland: Pathway Press, 1977), pp. 154-56.

Big Timber, Montana

For four years, Paul H. and Margaret Walker ministered among the Indians of the Northwest, many of them being saved, sanctified, and filled with the Holy Ghost. Among them was Mrs. Lillian (Little Soldier) Klaudt of the well known Klaudt Indian family.[18] This ministry extended to Big Timber, Montana, where today the Church of God has the Four Winds Ministry Center to Native Americans. In 1975, a young man and his wife answered a call to become missionaries to the Native Americans of Montana. For the past twenty-nine years, Ron and Kathy Countryman have faithfully and diligently served the nine tribes and seven reservations located in the remote and desolate areas of the Big Sky country, living in Big Timber, Montana. For the first twenty-four years, Ron and Kathy pastored small churches in the area and held a variety of positions. During this time, the Countrymans were building trust and confidence through their relationships with the Indian Nations.

In 1999, the Church of God World Missions Department, and in particular Bishop Roland Vaughn, made a momentous decision. The Countrymans would become recipients of direct assistance to help further their ministry and mission among the Native Americans. Bishop Vaughn, with his vast experience in working with Central American Indians, shared the burden with Ron and Kathy and helped develop a plan for training and teaching Native American pastors, associate pastors, and youth leaders to become more effective leaders and to disciple new converts. This concept of the fulfillment of the Great Commission included two elements: (1) the ministry must belong to the people, making them the foundation, and (2) the ministry must reproduce itself, not being dependent upon any one individual.

Through fund raising efforts by the World Missions Department and People for Care and Learning, twenty-five acres of land was purchased for the Four Winds Ministry Center. This property was formerly a truck stop and included a commercial kitchen and dining

---

[18] Walker, *Paths of a Pioneer*, p. 153. See also Corky Alexander, 'The Evangelistic Legacy of the Klaudt Indian Family', *Church of God Evangel* 100.6 (June 2010), p. 17.

facilities. Now the four Winds Ministry Center also has a chapel, dormitory, and classrooms for seminars and conferences.[19]

Pembroke, North Carolina

In 1948, R.P. Fields began missions among the Lumbee, Smiling, and Seminoles of Eastern North Carolina. A church was established at Saddletree, and from there, Pembroke. The ministry continued to grow, and in 1959 an impressive campground was erected.[20] I visited and ministered in Fields' church, and I cherish the friendship of Fields and his wife. His church in Laurinburg now has a Native American pastor.

Eagle Butte, South Dakota

Hilbert and Victor Nelson established their main ministry center in Eagle Butte, South Dakota, during the 1950s and 1960s. La Plant and Dupree congregations were later established.[21] I personally organized the project that helped to renovate the Eagle Butte Church of God building, which has in attendance members that are descendents of Chief Sitting Bull. The church is located on the Cheyenne River Reservation, the historic home of Chief Big Foot, who led his band to (and was killed at) Wounded Knee.

Gallup, New Mexico

W.M. Horton began the outreach that would become one of the largest Native American outreaches in the Church of God. Established at Two Wells, New Mexico, this Navajo and Zuni outreach began as an Indian camp meeting. Today, Southwest Indian Ministries, headquartered in Gallup, New Mexico, has dozens of churches among the Navajo and Zuni, and is an organized department under the umbrella of the Church of God USA Missions. A full-time director, who answers to a board, leads this ministry. The upcoming retirement of the director has stimulated desires for Native leadership.

---

[19] *Operation Compassion Partners with Montana Missionary* (Cleveland, TN: Operation Compassion, 2004).

[20] Conn, *Like a Mighty Army: A History of the Church of God*, pp. 399-400.

[21] Conn, *Like a Mighty Army: A History of the Church of God*, p. 400.

Anthropological Literature

Native Americans have been widely studied by anthropologists. Franz Boas, father of American anthropology,[22] spent a great deal of time researching the peoples of the Northwest Coast. His salvage ethnography[23] and historical particularism did much to further the idea that each culture has a unique history. This aids in the understanding of my context in that each Native American community, while it may be participating in inter-tribal gatherings, still continues to have a distinct tribal history and expressions of that culture. This is a critical reality, and while non-Natives need not try to ascertain the various cultural differences, it is important for any non-Native to keep in mind there are no universal tribal grids that can be applied, though some commonalities can be enjoyed in inter-tribal relationships.

Similarly, the California Indians were studied in depth by Alfred Louis Kroeber,[24] and his work on cultural areas[25] still influences the geographic and spatial understanding of the complex relationships of American Indian tribes. Ralph Linton published many pamphlets on the cultural practices of the Pawnee, who represent the Southern Plains cultural area. Though Linton used others' notes, and had not worked among the Pawnee himself, his contribution presents the life of these people and their ceremonial practices.[26] His work on tobacco must underlie any future work on the sacred pipe as it is beginning to be contextualized in a few Native churches.[27]

---

[22] E.g. see F. Boas and R. Benedict, *General Anthropology* (Boston, MA: Pub. for the US Armed forces institute by Heath, 1944).

[23] Salvage ethnography is a 'ethnography motivated by the need to obtain information about cultures threatened with extinction or assimilation' (P.A. Erickson and L.D. Murphy, *A History of Anthropological Theory* [Peterborough: Broadview Press, 2003], p. 183). This wide distribution of peoples deemed to be losing their culture contributes to the diversity of my study.

[24] A.L. Kroeber, *Handbook of the Indians of California* (Mineola, NY: Dover Pub., 1976).

[25] A.L. Kroeber, *Cultural and Natural Areas of Native North America* (Berkeley: University of California press, 1963).

[26] R. Linton, *Annual Ceremony of the Pawnee Medicine Men* (Chicago, IL: Field Museum of Natural History, 1923); *idem, The Thunder Ceremony of the Pawnee* (Chicago, IL: Field Museum of Natural History, 1922); *idem, The Sacrifice to the Morning Star by the Skidi Pawnee* (Chicago, IL: Field Museum of Natural History, 1922); *idem, Acculturation in Seven American Indian Tribes* (Gloucester: Peter Smith, 1963).

[27] R. Linton, *Use of Tobacco among North American Indians* (Chicago, IL: Field Museum of Natural History, 1924).

The anthropological significance of functionalism is important for my understanding of Native ceremony. I acknowledge that, in the experience of traditionalists, the practices and ceremonies themselves function in a traditional way before any Scripture or description is used to transform the meaning. For example, smudging functions as cleansing in the minds of First Nations people. This experience of cleansing would be available for any traditional person in the service, even if he or she does not embrace the new Christian meaning. Bronislaw Malinowski has provided an important work,[28] in which tribal practices are examined for the various functions that meet a variety of needs, and that maintain the community's homeostasis.

The functional aspect of rituals is addressed in this study as it aids in the understanding of the context in two ways. First, it sets forth that traditional Native practices meet particular needs in the community. They should not be prohibited simply because they do not appear in the historic Christian practices. Second, the theories regarding functionalism undergird the fact that a holistic ministry to a Native community cannot take place without an inclusion of these vital aspects of the community.

Symbolic Anthropology

Victor Turner's work on symbolism in rituals is helpful in analyzing ceremonial behavior of Native Americans.[29] Symbols such as smoke and drums have powerful significance for the traditional Native person entering a worship service. Turner demonstrates how to analyze the structure and properties of such symbols. A powerful effect and meaning present is in the early experience of the traditionalist attending a contextual service. Turner's symbolic approach aids in understanding the context of my study in the sense that it equips the untrained observer with a very important tool: knowledge that the strange practices that may make the observer afraid or prejudiced may be the very symbols that endear the gathering to traditional tribal peoples.

---

[28] B. Malinowski, *Argonauts of the Western Pacific* (Prospect Heights, IL: Waveland Press, 1984/1922).

[29] V.W. Turner, *The Forest of Symbols: Aspects of Ndembu Ritual* (Ithaca, NY: Cornell University Press, 1967).

Revitalization Movement Theory

Anthony F.C. Wallace and Paul G. Hiebert have written about revitalization movements and loom large in my consideration of contextualization.[30] Hiebert writes from both an anthropological and Christian perspective, and is regularly quoted by the Native American sources that I have utilized. The Native North American Contextual Movement can be called a revitalization movement, as it certainly revives certain practices in the cultures and fits with Wallace's definition. Wallace's view is based on Max Weber's concept that in times of social liminality, a charismatic prophet is needed to hold forth a new and truer worldview for the people.[31] What is even more helpful is the contextual aspect in which liminality results from social breakdown prompted by the impact of colonization. This helps us to understand the significance of the revitalization of Native ceremonies and practices.[32] It aids in understanding that there are the important motivations underlying the restoration of certain Native ceremonial practices that are vital to the health of the people and aid them in grappling with their painful history.

Nativistic Movement

Ralph Linton's helpful description of nativistic movements and acculturation provide an approach to analyzing an aspect of the Contextual Movement.[33] The Native American Contextual Movement cannot be considered a 'violent' movement, as one may call the Ghost Dance. As a non-violent nativistic movement, Linton would view the Contextual Movement as not trying to overcome the dominant culture, but merely seeking supernatural aid in coping with the domination.[34] Native Americans do not necessarily want to go back to all that they were in the past, but do want to recover certain aspects of their culture. Theoretical discussion aids in under-

---

[30] Anthony F.C. Wallace, 'Revitalization Movements', *American Anthropologist* 58 (1956), pp. 264-81; Paul G. Hiebert, *Anthropological Reflections on Missiological Issues* (Grand Rapids: Baker Books, 1994); *idem*, *Cultural Anthropology* (Grand Rapids: Baker Book House, 2nd edn, 1983); *idem*, *Anthropological Insights for Missionaries* (Grand Rapids: Baker Book House, 1985); Paul G. Hiebert, R. Daniel Shaw, and Tite Tiénou, *Understanding Folk Religion: A Christian Response to Popular Beliefs and Practices* (Grand Rapids: Baker Book House, 1999).
[31] Erickson and Murphy, *A History of Anthropological Theory*, pp. 111-12.
[32] Erickson and Murphy, *A History of Anthropological Theory*, pp. 111-12.
[33] Linton, *Acculturation in Seven American Indian Tribes*.
[34] Linton, *Acculturation in Seven American Indian Tribes*, p. 518.

standing the context and removing the fear of contextualization being driven by political motivations. It is not that Native Americans do not appreciate the work of sincere missionaries or that they want to overthrow denominations or government, but rather that they desire to recover their traditions as a part of their healing and coping processes, both individually and collectively.

Pan-Indianism Theory

James Howard, who believed that Pan-Indianism was a final step that immediately preceded total assimilation,[35] was a source for the more recent and pertinent work of William K. Powers[36] in his consideration of inter-tribal movements.[37] Powers believes that the mutual exchange of tribal cultural practices in an inter-tribal expression will lead to the dissolution of tribal identity to form one group, 'American Indian'. His hypothesis, however, underestimates the complexity of tribal culture.[38] Powers informs my study with a helpful analysis of Pan-Indianism, assimilation, and inter-tribalism. Pan-Indianism and inter-tribalism are important concepts for understanding the context, and provide insight on the complex relationships of differing tribes that have common songs, dances, and approaches to the drum, as well as other common cultural practices that help bring scattered tribes together for community experiences important for the healing of Indian communities. Despite having common practices, individual tribal symbols are present during their mutual ceremonies so that no tribe's uniqueness is lost. All of this underscores the fact that Indians can gather together in inter-tribal expressions without losing their tribal identities.

---

[35] J.H. Howard, 'Pan-Indian Culture of Oklahoma', *The Scientific Monthly* 81.5 (1955), pp. 215-20.

[36] William K. Powers, *Beyond the Vision: Essays on American Indian Culture* (Norman, OK: University of Oklahoma Press, 1987); *idem, Oglala Religion* (Lincoln: University of Nebraska Press, 1977); *idem, Yuwipi: Vision and Experience in Oglala Ritual* (Lincoln, NE: University of Nebraska Press, 1982); *idem, Wardance: Plains Indian Musical Performance* (Tuscon, AZ: The University of Arizona Press, 1990).

[37] William K. Powers, 'Native American Music of the Twentieth Century', in Robert Santelli, Holly George-Warren, and Jim Brown (eds.), *American Roots Music* (New York: Harry N. Abrams, 2001), pp. 144-59.

[38] Powers, *Wardance: Plains Indian Musical Performance*, p. 108.

Theological Literature

Theological sources include a range of Pentecostal theologies, missiological volumes, and texts on the theology of religions. Non-Native sources tend to follow a systematic rather than a narrative form (which is more Native), with a few exceptions. The following are helpful for understanding the contextual Pentecostal Native environment.

Redemptive Analogy

Native Americans have recognized the value of Don Richardson's concept of redemptive analogy, a concept which may be partially responsible for the selection of representative biblical texts that certain Natives use to defend their positions on contextualization. The two works most impacting Native Americans are *Peace Child,* originally published in 1974, and *Eternity in Their Hearts,* published in 1984.[39] Richardson's concept of 'redemptive analogy' serves as an interpretive paradigm, but is weak for my purposes for at least three reasons. First, he is a white missionary and does not explain contextualization from an indigenous perspective; second, his context is not Native North America; and third, he does not approach his theory from a Pentecostal perspective *per se.* His approach is, however, biblical, and he grounds his work on the Acts of the Apostles, placing him in a Pentecostal arena. I include him primarily because several of my subjects use his work.

The concept of redemptive analogy arises from Paul's words at Mars Hill recorded in Acts (Acts 17.22-31), in which the Apostle points to ideas within the culture and quotes poets of the culture to use as an object lesson to teach the eternal truths of the gospel of Jesus Christ. The idea assumes that God is already at work in pre-Christian cultures to establish paradigmatic symbols that can be used to illustrate the plan of salvation and other truths about the Creator. This aids in understanding my context where Richardson's ideas are already in use.

---

[39] D. Richardson, *Peace Child* (Ventura, CA: Regal Books, 1974); *idem, Eternity in Their Hearts* (Ventura, CA: Regal books, 1984).

Pentecostal Theology

Works by Pentecostal theologians include Walter Hollenweger,[40] Harvey Cox, Clark Pinnock, John Christopher Thomas, Kimberly Alexander, Amos Yong, and Veli-Matti Kärkkäinen. They represent the development of a growing body of Pentecostal scholarship that features dimensions that can also be found in an indigenous theology. They include discernment from a spiritual approach rather than a solely scriptural approach, oral liturgy, narrative theology, inclusion of dreams and visions, and the use of sacred objects.[41] For Pentecostals, sacred objects include anointing oil, water for footwashing, and prayer cloths. The works by these authors aid in understanding the context because the churches observed and the persons interviewed were Pentecostal. It is also significant because it is this use of sacred objects that some individuals find objectionable and thus prohibit contextualized Native practices.

The focus of this research upon Native Pentecostals was not intentional, but rather lies in the fact that almost all of the leaders of the Native American contextual movement have connections to Pentecostalism, if not being Pentecostal themselves. It is only reasonable to identify what parts of their activity is Pentecostal and what is Native. This aids in understanding the context as they speak and act in Pentecostal ways.

Theology of Religions

Moving beyond a belief that traditional practices can be modified and utilized in Christian worship and ministry, a theology of religions allows for the possibility that God is actively at work in other

---

[40] W.J. Hollenweger, *The Pentecostals* (London: SCM, 1972); *idem*, *Pentecostalism: Origins and Developments Worldwide* (Peabody, MA: Hendrickson Publishers, 1997); H. Cox, *Fire from Heaven: The Rise of Pentecostal Spirituality and the Reshaping of Religion in the Twenty-First Century* (Reading, MA: Addison Wesley Publishing Company, 1994); C.H. Pinnock, *Flame of Love: A Theology of the Holy Spirit* (Downers Grove: InterVarsity Press, 1999); John Christopher Thomas, *Footwashing in the Gospel of John and the Johannine Community* (JSNTSup, 61; Sheffield: JSOT Press, 1991); *idem*, *The Spirit of the New Testament* (Blandford Forum, UK: Deo Publishing, 2005); Kimberly Ervin Alexander, *Pentecostal Healing: Models in Theology and Practice* (JPTSup, 29; Blandford Forum, UK: Deo Publishing, 2006); A. Yong, *Discerning the Spirit(s): A Pentecostal-Charismatic Contribution to Christian Theology of Religions* (JPTSup, 20; Sheffield: Sheffield Academic Press, 2000); V.M. Kärkkäinen, *An Introduction to the Theology of Religions: Biblical, Historical and Contemporary Perspectives* (Downers Grove: InterVarsity Press, 2003).

[41] Hollenweger, *Pentecostalism: Origins and Developments Worldwide*, p. 19.

religions. William Stolzman's *The Pipe and Christ: A Christian-Sioux Dialogue* is an interesting attempt at developing a Sioux/Catholic contextualization.[42] However, though an experienced missionary, Stolzman is a non-Native. His may be an early attempt at a theology of religions approach to contextualization, but because his work is structured around Catholic ritual practices relating to the sacred pipe, and the fact that tobacco has been rejected by my primary audience, it will not serve my purposes here.

Veli-Matti Kärkkäinen and Amos Yong are the two most important voices for theology of religions that aid in understanding my context.[43] Yong is especially helpful in his pneumatological approach that includes 'mediating categories'. These categories include religious experience, religious utility, and religious cosmology.[44] This is helpful in that it begins as interfaith dialogue, acknowledging that the Creator is already in the religion, and speaks from the premise of the Great Spirit first, thus avoiding an impasse. The emphasis on cosmology is helpful as the earth is extremely important to Native Americans. A theology of religions helps to understand the context of the religious landscape in the Indian community.

Missiological Literature

My inclusion and interaction with the missiological sources reflects either their presence in the discussions of Native Americans as they describe contextualization or the relative importance that I feel the theories hold for the analysis I am doing. The most important of these sources are the works authored by Hiebert, Shaw, Van Engen, and Tiénou.[45] The model I will employ for critical contextu-

---

[42] William Stolzman, *The Pipe and Christ: A Christian-Sioux Dialogue* (Chamberlin: Tipi Press, 6th edn, 1998).

[43] Kärkkäinen, *An Introduction to the Theology of Religions*; Yong, *Discerning the Spirit(s)*. See also Tony Richie, *Speaking by the Spirit: A Pentecostal Model for Interreligious Dialogue* (Lexington, KY: Emeth Press, 2011); *idem*, 'Approaching the Problem of Religious Truth in a Pluralistic World: A Pentecostal-Charismatic Contribution', *Journal of Ecumenical Studies* 43.3 (2008), pp. 351-69; *idem*, 'God's Fairness to People of All Faiths: A Respectful Proposal to Pentecostals for Discussion Regarding World Religions', *Pneuma* 28.1 (2006), pp. 105-119; *idem*, 'Revamping Pentecostal Evangelism: Appropriating Walter J. Hollenweger's Radical Proposal', *International Review of Mission* 96.382-383 (2007), pp. 343-54.

[44] Yong, *Discerning the Spirit(s)*, p. 222.

[45] Hiebert, *Anthropological Insights for Missionaries*; *idem*, *Anthropological Reflections on Missiological Issues*; R.D. Shaw and C.E. Van Engen, *Communicating God's Word in*

alization will draw more from works of Hiebert, Shaw, and Tiénou. I will modify this model with Pentecostal aspects to help analyze further what Pentecostal Native Americans are doing in their worship services. It is necessary, at this point to review Hiebert's four steps to critical contextualization:

1. phenomenological examination;
2. testing beliefs and practices in light of biblical truth and tests of reality;
3. evaluating old beliefs and practices in the light of biblical truth;
4. advancing ministries that transform individuals and congregations from where they are to where God wants them to be.[46]

Hiebert's model for critical contextualization has served as an essential tool for missionaries studying the biblical and theological world of mission as well as for studying the beliefs of people who are the object of mission. The model envisions a missionary and a 'target group' working together prayerfully, with the aid of Scripture, to come to critically important conclusions concerning the addition of various cultural practices into the Christian worship of the people.

The importance of Hiebert's model cannot be overstated in the light of the age-old dualism into which people groups fall, allowing cultural practices to slip underground and be practiced in secret uncritically because they conflict with church standards. Hiebert's model has served effectively in countless missionary contexts as a landmark aid. It appears to be ideally effective in a traditional setting where there is limited knowledge of Christian doctrine and practice.[47]

Also important to the ceremonies and practices in the context of this study are the contributions of Sherwood Lingenfelter.[48] The indigenous people I describe do not need to overcome many of the

---

a Complex World: God's Truth or Hocus Pocus? (Lanham, MD: Rowman & Littlefield, 2003); Hiebert, Shaw, and Tiénou: *Understanding Folk Religion.*

[46] Hiebert, Shaw, and Tiénou, *Understanding Folk Religion*, pp. 369-92.

[47] Hiebert, Shaw, and Tiénou, *Understanding Folk Religion*, pp. 369-92.

[48] Sherwood Lingenfelter, *Transforming Culture: A Challenge for Christian Mission* (Grand Rapids: Baker Book House, 1998); *idem, Agents of Transformation: A Guide for Effective Cross-Cultural Ministry* (Grand Rapids: Baker Book House, 1996).

cultural biases of traditional missionaries. However, their use of Scripture, contextualized language, and contextualized ministry strategies certainly corresponds with Lingenfelter's idea of *Agents of Transformation*. Shaw and Van Engen's helpful volume taught me how language is at once a complex and effective vehicle for gospel communication.[49]

Native Voices

In surveying the literature that would be helpful for understanding my context, it was very encouraging to discover a number of Native authors in the fields of history, theology, and missiology. Some of these authors, such as Vine Deloria, expressed quite frankly their perspective on why the field of anthropology does not have more Native authors.[50]

Historical Literature
Native American histories detail important missionaries such as Evan Jones, who, according to Randy Woodley (Keetoowah Cherokee)[51] in his work on diversity, allowed a stomp dance to be performed on church property.[52] The emergence of Native American scholars like Woodley, commenting on history, is coming into its own. Clara Sue Kidwell's *Choctaws and Missionaries in Mississippi, 1818-1918* is important in that rather than focusing on detailed accounts of contextualized practices during the time of Indian removal, it reflects the impact of European ethos.[53] Histories authored by Native Americans serve to underscore what Vine Deloria's (Standing Rock Sioux) work (another important indigenous history) declares concerning itself:

> [T]he Indian task of keeping an informed public available to assist the tribes in their efforts to survive is never ending, and so

---

[49] Shaw and Van Engen, *Communicating God's Word in a Complex World: God's Truth or Hocus Pocus?*

[50] Vine Deloria, Jr., *Custer Died for Your Sins: An Indian Manifesto* (Norman, OK: University of Oklahoma Press, 1989/1969), pp. 78-100.

[51] In this study I will at first mention and often cite the Native American individual's tribal membership in parentheses after his/her name.

[52] Randy Woodley, *Living in Color: Embracing God's Passion for Ethnic Diversity* (Downers Grove, IL: InterVarsity Press, 2001), p. 128.

[53] Kidwell, *Choctaws and Missionaries in Mississippi, 1818-1918*.

the central message of this book, that Indians are alive, have certain dreams of their own, and are being overrun by the ignorance and the mistaken, misdirected efforts of those who would help them, can never be repeated too often.[54]

Theological Literature

There is an ever increasing stream of Native people writing theology that reflects an Indian perspective. This is marked by the publication of a volume of distinctively Native American theology, which approaches theology spatially rather than temporally,[55] answering Deloria's cry for such a work. Sadly, the work is systematic, rather than narrative.[56] Representatives of several tribes authored this publication. This aspect alone makes it fascinating in its treatment of Christian theology from varied tribal perspectives. The strongest aspect of the work is the spatial approach. This challenges my historical orientation and forces me to bring the sacred places into the discussions of the ceremonies.

The presence of a distinctively Native American theological journal, the *Journal of North American Institute for Indigenous Theological Studies* (NAIITS), edited by leaders of the Native American Contextual Movement, may be the most important piece of literature serving as the background for my study. I was able to glean much from its volumes for my research. In it I have been able to observe what is really different about the Native approach to writing theology. Natives write with an emphasis on narrative and orality and incorporate a spatial approach. The challenge for my purposes has been that when Native Americans begin writing theology, they do so simply from the standpoint of a Native writing theology, not to explain the details of practices that are not intended to be gawked at

---

[54] Deloria, *Custer Died for Your Sins: An Indian Manifesto*, p. xiii.

[55] C.S. Kidwell, H. Noley, and G.E. Tinker, *Native American Theology* (Maryknoll, NY: Orbis Books, 2001). When I speak of a temporal approach, I mean an approach that describes significance and reality more in terms of a historical context than through significance of place. Vine Deloria said, 'In a world in which communications are nearly instantaneous and simultaneous experiences are possible, it must be spaces and places that distinguish us from each other, not time nor history' (*God Is Red*, p. 65).

[56] Since this volume's release there are a number of Native American theologians framing their theology in terms of narrative. Richard Twiss' dissertation is an example ('Native-led Contextualization Efforts in North America, 1989-2009').

or probed by non-Natives. My weakness is that I am not a Native American, and I can only tell the story from my outside perspective – and we need their story!

There is a paucity of theological works authored by Native Americans (other than those by Deloria and Kidwell), and other sources authored by Natives interested in contextualization are written on a more popular level. A redeeming factor, however, is that a number of the authors are now in their dissertation phase of doctoral studies or have completed their degrees – for example, Richard Twiss,[57] Randy Woodley,[58] and Adrian Jacobs.[59] Papers from the *Missio Dei* conference in Nashville, Tennessee (2006), along with papers written by leaders of the Contextual Movement were also helpful resources. I have tried to honor these leaders and their words. The weakness of these sources is that although a number of them are Pentecostal, they do not write or critique their movement and practices from a Pentecostal perspective. I will engage the dissertation of only one subject of my interviews and participant observations, Cheryl Bear-Barnetson.[60] She is distinctively and unashamedly a Pentecostal scholar. This aided me in understanding my context, as Bear-Barnetson exercises a Native Pentecostal hermeneutic that is integrated with redemptive analogy.

Missiological Literature

The volume by Twiss entitled *Dancing Our Prayers* demonstrates the ongoing discussion concerning syncretistic possibilities in inclusion of Native American traditional practices.[61] I include it here because Twiss himself is a missiologist and uses missiological sources to support his argument. In it, Twiss defends what he believes is an erroneous critique of his writings in an official document of The Christian and Missionary Alliance. While, as Twiss clarifies, it is im-

---

[57] Richard Twiss, *One Church Many Tribes: Following Jesus the Way God Made You* (Ventura, CA: Regal, 2000); *idem, Dancing Our Prayers.*

[58] Woodley, *Living in Color*; and Randy Woodley, *When Going to Church Is Sin and Other Essays on Native American Christian Missions* (Garden City: Morgan James, 2007).

[59] Adrian Jacobs, *Aboriginal Christianity: The Way It Was Meant to Be* (Rapid City, SD: Adrian Jacobs, 1998).

[60] Cheryl Bear-Barnetson, 'Introduction to First Nations Ministry: Everything One Wants to Know, but Is Afraid They Are Too White to Ask' (Professional Ministry Research Project, The King's Seminary, 2009).

[61] Twiss, *Dancing Our Prayers.*

portant to be wary of the demonization of certain religious objects, it is sad that the Christian and Missionary Alliance made a broad and sweeping prohibition of redeeming Native sacred objects, in the light of the fact that it's founder, A.B. Simpson, was closely associated with Pentecostalism, a movement that has been known for the use of sacred objects. This helps me to understand my context by allowing me to listen in on a Native defending his position and the right to contextualize. I turn now to the historical material by Native writers regarding the specific practices that are pertinent to this study.

Historical Background of Specific Native American Traditional Practices

Literature I found helpful in ascertaining the historical background of specific practices included histories, encyclopedias, and monographs that discuss the history of Native American practices. The most beneficial of these volumes were the encyclopedias by Green and Fernandez[62] and Lyon.[63]

Language

The most commonly contextualized practice in Native American Pentecostal churches, as in all Native American Christian churches, is the use of indigenous language. This makes language an interesting entry point for understanding Native American contextualization, since language is an important window to the culture as a whole.

Prior to European contact, there were at least 2,200 Indian languages to be found in approximately twelve distinct linguistic groups throughout North America. The more classic Native American histories discuss these linguist issues.[64] There were a multiplied number of tribes, and many Native people spoke several languages. Those languages included sign and trade languages.

Missionaries and the government led a cultural assault on Native languages, forbidding the speaking of those languages in schools

---

[62] Rayna Green and Melanie Fernandez, *The British Museum Encyclopedia of Native North America* (Bloomington, IN: Indiana University Press, 1999).

[63] W.S. Lyon, *Encyclopedia of Native American Healing* (New York: WW Norton & Company, 1998).

[64] Wilson, *The Earth Shall Weep: A History of Native America*; A.M. Josephy, *The Indian Heritage of America* (Wilmington, MA: Mariner Books, 1991), p. 4.

and even on the reservations. For a few peoples, such as the Cherokee, development of a written language (Sequoyan) was combined with the rare support of the Church in using the tribal language in a religious context, in order to keep the language alive. Language was usually the main target for those who wished Indians to 'assimilate' and 'be civilized'.[65]

Many languages died out in the 17th century, along with the people who spoke them, but recent advances, in conjunction with such moves as the Cherokee Language and Culture Preservation Bill, have empowered Native peoples to work to preserve their languages. Only a few tribes have written language, such as the Cherokee, but language continues to be preserved through 'song, story and dance'.[66] Though I consulted several reliable linguistic sources, I was unable to identify a specific number of extant Native American languages.

Smudging

Smudging is the practice that holds the most significance for the Pentecostal movement in my study, due to the importance of fire as a symbol of the Holy Spirit and the presence of fire language even in Pentecostal doctrinal formulations (such as, 'baptism with the Holy Ghost and fire'). In a purely traditional use, smudging is also used to cleanse sacred objects, as well as individuals.[67] Yet, smudging is also the most controversial practice that I have included in this study.[68] This is somewhat surprising to be so, in the light of a long tradition of incense in both the Roman Catholic and Eastern Orthodox traditions, not to mention the Old and New Testaments. Bear-Barnetson gives a historical definition in her unpublished dissertation.

> Native people have a ceremony called the Smudge. This is a cleansing or purification ceremony that cleanses body, soul, and spirit. Lighting sage, sweet grass, or cedar and then blowing out

---

[65] Green and Fernandez, *The British Museum Encyclopedia of Native North America*, p. 90.

[66] Green and Fernandez, *The British Museum Encyclopedia of Native North America*, p. 91.

[67] Lyon, *Encyclopedia of Native American Healing*, p. 201.

[68] I am not discussing this in order of most to least controversial but rather in order of most common to least common usage (though this could be debated).

the fire cause it to smoke in a large abalone shell. The person who desires cleansing pulls the smoke onto them and washes with it. The smell of the sage, sweet grass or cedar is very pungent to those unaccustomed to it but to the indigenous people it is a beautiful scent (Malachi 1:11).[69]

Bear-Barnetson's historical definition is most important in the literature I examined, due to the fact that she and her husband are both subjects of my participant observations and interviewees. Being Native Pentecostal pastors, they give a definition of smudging which helps guide my analysis. The American Indian Contextual Movement gives the following case as an example of the historic ceremony of smudging in the theological journal of the contextual movement.

> Suppose a Greek Christian enjoys the fragrant cinnamon aroma of a burning candle or sandalwood incense. She enjoys the fragrance purely for its aesthetic value. Now suppose that she finds it personally meaningful to occasionally burn the candle or incense during her devotional prayer time. For her, it brings to mind the Scripture in Revelation that depicts prayer as incense, symbolically and literally, rising up to the very throne of God for His pleasure. The smell and smoke symbolically reminds her that through faith in Jesus Christ, God hears and answers prayer. Can you see anything wrong with this picture? Now change the scenario and imagine that it is a Native Christian who enjoys the fragrant aroma of burning sage, sweet grass, or cedar – in effect incense. Again, imagine that this Native believer is also symbolically reminded by the sight of the ascending smoke, and aroma of the burning cedar bark, that prayers, through faith in Jesus Christ, are literally ascending upward to the very presence of God. The smoke and smell is a symbol or picture of the prayers of the saints spoken of in the Bible. Can you see anything wrong with this picture?[70]

This official statement in a theological journal underscores the cultural importance of smudging among Native Americans and de-

---

[69] Bear-Barnetson, 'Introduction to First Nations Ministry', p. 158.

[70] Adrian Jacobs, Richard Twiss, and Terry Leblanc, 'Culture, Christian Faith and Error', *The Journal of the North American Institute for Indigenous Theological Studies* 1.1 (2003), p. 33.

scribes the general symbolic interpretation that can be correlated to Scripture. The statement is clearly intended by the movement to take smudging out of the realm of dangerous syncretistic practice and place it in comparison to orthodox Christian practice. The popularity of smudging, both in Native American contexts and Native Pentecostal churches, prompts me to recognize this important practice (see Chapter 3).

Drums and Rattles

Once a significant issue, the allowance of drums and percussion instruments in local church worship has been less of an issue in the so-called 'worship wars' since the 1970s in the United States. The gathering drum is equally as controversial as smudging in a few Indian contexts where people emphasize that the drum has its own spirit. Still, the stereotypical warnings about 'African rhythms' dominate much of the criticisms of Native American drum usage.[71] Participants in the Native American Contextual Movement can discuss with clarity the importance of drums and rattles in Christian worship. Richard Twiss deals with the subject in his works.[72]

The Native American gathering drum, medicine drum, or 'big drum', can be found in many American Indian traditions. It made its way into the powwow and today is a very important aspect of the contextualized Native American worship service. Historically, in Native traditions, the drum is believed to have a life of its own. Every drum has its own breath and voice and must be taken care of by a special designated 'drum keeper'. Although historically women have not participated in drum teams, changing times have witnessed women sitting at the drum.[73] These beliefs concerning the drum have made its presence in churches controversial.

Hand drums and rattles often accompany 'big drum' usage and similar issues accompany their inclusion. The various visions Native Americans possess surrounding the drum have dictated the way drums are decorated, and this practice is also being contextualized in American Indian and First Nation churches.

---

[71] Twiss, *One Church Many Tribes*, p. 117.

[72] Twiss, *One Church Many Tribes*; idem, *Dancing Our Prayers*.

[73] Green and Fernandez, *The British Museum Encyclopedia of Native North America*, p. 56.

Dance

Also coming to Native peoples through the medium of dreams and visions are the dances, many associated with ceremonies, expressing the 'relationships between people, animals and the spirits of the world'.[74] Many of these dances are social and have been incorporated into contemporary powwow dances that are used in performance and competition. Many others are vitally connected to seasons and the land, illustrating the need for spatial considerations. For example, a Hopi Rain Dance is irrelevant apart from the local climate and situation to which the dance applies.[75] Wilson's work contains a helpful discussion of dance and its connection to Native worldview.[76]

Some of the classic mission histories reflect non-Native understanding and are, in part, responsible for a negative view of Native dancing. Because dances of Native American and First Nations people are often connected with larger ceremonies,[77] they are attached to other behaviors that are strange and even frightening to non-Natives. Those not understanding the larger social and religious functions of the ceremony have tended to avoid or prohibit Native dancing altogether.[78]

Contemporary powwow dancing has developed out of traditional dances, and has been revived as Native people have gone off to war. Many Native American ceremonies functioned as preparation for wartime conflict and healing from its consequences. Dance is no exception. During World War I, the patriotic aspects of the powwow increased, and today powwows cover the landscape of Indian country, featuring the various dances characteristic of the powwow tradition. Twiss's book, *Dancing Our Prayers*, reveals the strength of the view of dancing as prayer in the history of the contextual movement.

---

[74] Green and Fernandez, *The British Museum Encyclopedia of Native North America*, p. 52.

[75] Deloria, *God Is Red*, p. 70.

[76] Wilson, *The Earth Shall Weep: A History of Native America*, p. 7.

[77] Some Native ceremonies are referred to simply as dances, such as Green Corn Dance, Booger Dance, Stomp Dance, and so on.

[78] Paul G. Hiebert and Frances F. Hiebert, *Case Studies in Missions* (Grand Rapids, MI: Baker Book House, 1987), pp. 103-108.

Talking Circles

The following definition is in keeping with the understanding of talking circles that I have experienced in my participant observations:

> The talking circle as we know it today is a modern version of what was once called the council fire. Council fires were usually called by a member of the tribe who was wrestling with a problem, and needed the advice of the elders and medicine people. Today's talking circle is used in a number of different ways. For instance, a memorial hospital in Arizona conducts a weekly talking circle for Native Americans with diabetes from a nearby Indian reservation in an effort to combine traditional with Western medical treatment; Alaskan students at a multicultural education conference used the talking circle to share ideas about how to preserve language and culture; and talking circles are used by various faiths for interfaith dialogues.[79]

The symbol of the circle is not lost on Native people who see it as a symbol of the whole family of life and the consensus of inter-human discourse[80] as well as a symbol of de-centralized leadership.[81]

The Importance of Ceremony

Unlike Euro-Americans, who separate their lives into compartmentalized categories such as 'sacred' and 'secular', Indians treat the whole of life as sacred and consequently reveal all of life to be 'religious' through these practices that are at once both spatial and cyclical, rather than temporal.[82] An example is that of Johnson Dennison's beautiful description of the traditional Navajo Enemy Way Ceremony (see Appendix A). He describes the historical significance of the Enemy Way Ceremony. Native American ceremonies are numerous, and serve as extensions of the everyday life of the tribal peoples.

---

[79] F.D. Feather and R. Robinson, *Exploring Native American Wisdom: Lore, Traditions, and Rituals That Connect Us All* (Franklin Lakes, NJ: Career Press, 2003), p. 113.

[80] H. Owusu, *Symbols of Native America* (New York: Sterling, 1999), p. 24.

[81] O. Brafman and R.A. Beckstrom, *The Starfish and the Spider: The Unstoppable Power of Leaderless Organizations* (New York: Portfolio, 2006), pp. 19-20.

[82] Kidwell, Noley, and Tinker, *Native American Theology*, pp. 12-13.

Summary

The state of literature concerning Native American Christianity is at a point of transition from a Euro-American scientific and temporal body of work to a body of literature that features Native American voices speaking of Christianity in more spatial terms. This more adequately reflects Native American worldviews. I am fortunate to be able to feature some of these voices in my study and lift up their interests. Out of honor for the Native traditions, I seriously considered framing this work in ways that would reflect their narrative and spatial approaches. However, the overriding constraints of the academy have caused me to settle for a more Euro-American approach. I have, however, attempted to approach the case studies from the standpoint of their respective cultural areas, and in doing so include anthropological voices that have previously written about Native Americans. While historical sources from more of a military history perspective have been considered, fresh voices of a pneumatological theology of religions will be integrated with some of the helpful theories to be found in anthropological and missiological sources.

2

METHODOLOGY

> Are ceremonies restricted to particular places, and do they become useless in a foreign land? These questions have never been critically examined within Western religious circles, because of the preemption of temporal considerations by Christian theology.[1]

The study of Native ceremonies is one that will evolve over time as Natives take charge of the historical, anthropological, and missiological disciplines. Although the following methodology reflects less of a spatial approach, it does reflect one that acknowledges sensitivity to Native concerns.

Qualitative Research

My use of qualitative data is important to me for several reasons. I concur with Tony Wigram's explanation of qualitative research as focusing on how something works, not just that it does work.[2] The newness of the American Indian Contextual Movement prevents me from having a large enough sample to do effective quantitative research, but it is possible to examine how these practices are working in Native American Pentecostal churches.

---

[1] Deloria, *God Is Red*, p. 71.
[2] See Tony Wigram, Inge Nygaard Pedersen, and Lars Ole Bonde, *A Comprehensive Guide to Music Therapy: Theory, Clinical Practice, Research, and Training* (London: Jessica Kingsley Publishers, 2002).

Participant Observation

The initial qualitative research data I work with is largely biblical, historical, and archival. It is in this portion of the research that I reviewed the meaning of ritual religious practice among Native Americans. I also intentionally planned in my research to spend some time at various Native American churches observing worship services where different traditional practices were employed. Participant observation is important in order to validate the actual context and provide a framework for asking questions directly related to my observation experience – what Shaw calls the 'observation-questioning technique'.[3] Further interviews of participants revealed the meaning and significance that these practices hold for these individuals and the communities they represent.

My field research took place in several different cultural areas and resulted in seven case studies in which I observed and evaluated Native American worship services utilizing traditional Native practices for their spiritual benefit and transformational power. This was done at Bear-Barnetson and Barnetson's First Nations Foursquare Church, in Santa Fe Springs, California; Window Rock Church of God (Navajo) in Window Rock, Arizona; Sacred Ground Outreach in Siletz, Oregon; and with Larry 'Grizz' Brown (Creek/Cherokee) at his Living Way Chapel Foursquare Church, in Apple Valley, California. Other important visits were to Bacone College in Muskogee, Oklahoma, where I met with Kyle Taylor (Pawnee/Choctaw); The Azusa Centennial Native American Gathering at the Los Angeles Convention Center; Eagle Butte Church of God, Eagle Butte, South Dakota; and Cherokee Church of God, Cherokee, North Carolina. I wanted to do this in order to understand whether the use of traditional practices is perceived to be beneficial for Native Christian spirituality or whether they should be 'left in Egypt'.[4]

---

[3] R. Daniel Shaw, *Transculturation: The Cultural Factor in Translation and Other Communication Tasks* (Pasadena, CA: William Carey Library, 1988), p. 42.

[4] One argument for not using tradition is that the old traditions do not exist any longer, or the people have no memory of them (Tarango, '"Choosing the Jesus Way:" the Assemblies of God's Home Missions to American Indians and the Development of a Pentecostal Indian Identity', p. 166). This was not true of my interviewees.

I acknowledge that there are possible liabilities to the validity of this research due to the participatory nature of spiritual experiences and the objective judgments that worship leaders make in a given context. I have felt, however, that it is time for non-Natives and non-traditional Natives alike to begin to try to understand, in whatever limited way, the importance of traditional cultural practices people actually use and why we need to welcome these experiences into local churches.

Personal Interviews

Through a total of eleven personal interviews I focused on two basic questions: 'What traditional practices do you presently contextualize in your worship services?' and 'How does it make you feel to worship in a Native way?' From those starting points the interviewees departed in any number of directions and I followed the lead of my interviewees. This lack of directed communication led to discovering the importance of at least two practices (language and smudging) that I had not expected to include. I had six telephone interviews and five interviews done in person. Because I interviewed an individual on the telephone did not mean, however, that I had not previously conducted an interview in person. Time with a pastor following a worship service is limited, and it was a benefit for the interview to take place later on the telephone. In one case, the end of one face-to-face interview raised awareness of a practice about which I later called back and discussed with the pastor on the telephone.

Collection of Data

My participant observations are documented in hand-written field notes taken either during the service, or immediately thereafter. Initially, I had planned to do some video recording, but at the *Missio Dei* Gathering in Nashville, Tennessee, I witnessed a conversation between Casey Church (a Native pastor) and a Native American cameraman that changed my plan. My feeling was that if there were a ceremony that was not allowed to be video recorded, it would be a barrier and limitation to my research. I did elect to utilize DVDs that were recorded and produced for distribution by Native Americans themselves of the Azusa Street Native American Gathering. These represent services that I attended and in which I did participant observation, but which featured observation foci of Native Americans themselves.

All but one of the interviews was recorded using the computer program 'Garage Band' and a Mac iBook G4. The recording of these audio interviews progressed from initially using a Realistic telephone recorder, then moving to Skype, which had a much higher quality. The recording quality of the Skype telephone interviews is close to that of a radio interview, complete with reverb.

The face-to-face interviews were recorded on the same Mac iBook G4 into Garage Band, utilizing a built-in microphone on the computer. This quality was inferior due to low volume levels and the soft vocal tones of some Native Americans in contrast to the flat and louder Southern voices similar to my own.

All of the interviews were transcribed by a paid transcriber and loaded into one Microsoft Word document, which made them searchable. I then coded certain sections that represented recurring themes and issues. I marked the thematic codes by using the 'comment' function in the correction tool, and then pulled them back up with the 'find' function to see the relationships between the coded data.

Data Analysis

Data analysis enabled me to answer my second and third research questions: 'How do Native American traditional practices enhance Pentecostal worship?' and 'In what way are traditional practices helpful in Native American Pentecostal worship and witness?' The thematic coding of the field notes aided me in both adjusting Hiebert's model to describe what is going on and to supplement the description with any other aspects that are vital to understanding Native American behavior. My inclusion of long quotes from the personal interviews is one way I am giving voice to Native Americans who are rarely heard describing their own ceremonial behavior.

Limitations

The limitations of such a study are somewhat paradoxical. On the one hand, my primary Euro-American orientation has made it difficult for me to comprehend fully the experiential impact of these practices due to my cultural conditioning. On the other hand, such a study is highly subjective in that it attempts to evaluate worship experiences that are extremely spiritual and value-laden for participants. This limitation was answered by the words of the worshipers themselves, who gladly described to me what they felt was happening. Pentecostal worship, however, holds much to witness both visually and orally, and is more conducive to observation than other more quietist expressions of Christianity. The fact that my interview questions are not sufficiently specific to guide a deliberate discussion may be considered a limitation, but the strength of this approach is that they leave the interviewee free to discuss the aspects of the subject that are of special interest to them.

Another limitation arose during my follow-up telephone calls. In some instances interviewees felt it necessary to explain a particular practice that they assumed I was interested in, but in most instances they were interested in talking about the practice that was their own particular interest, because they knew I understood their focus.

The geographic and cultural variation of the tribal contexts may also be seen as a liability to the validity of the conclusions, but I made every effort to analyze each practice within its specific (and often tribal) context, except in cases where the groups refer to each other or share a common approach to a practice.

PART TWO

CEREMONIALISM: ITS PRACTICE
AND MEANING

3

PRACTICES THAT REVEAL NATIVE AMERICAN BELIEFS AND VALUES

In this chapter my intention is to detail the significant practices that are being utilized by worshiping Pentecostal Christians in contexts across the Native American experience. The focus is on participant observation in Muskogee, Oklahoma; Santa Fe Springs, California; Apple Valley, California; Window Rock, Arizona; and Siletz, Oregon. Throughout this process I utilized Hiebert's critical contextualization process, modified by a pneumatological Pentecostal theology of religions. This resulted in description of the transformed practice within a particular ecclesiastical context. The significant practices include language, smudging, use of drums and rattles, dance, talking circles, and ceremony.

As I present these various Native American practices, I will follow an order and format similar to Hiebert's critical contextualization theory. This will enable the reader to appreciate the nature of the data I collected. What follows is a presentation of data relating these practices to ceremony as a manifestation of Native approaches to the supernatural.

Language

And everyone present was filled with the Holy Spirit and began speaking in other languages, as the Holy Spirit gave them this ability (Acts 2.4).

My observations of Native American language in worship services had a significant impact upon the direction of my analysis. I began this study with a polarized view. Due to the controversial nature of drumming and smudging, I was distracted from noticing that a worship service using only traditional language still had a high degree of Native American perspective that impacted the worship experience. Thanks to Taylor, I was able to include a few churches that I might have considered not to be 'contextual'.[1]

Practice Description

The churches that I observed varied in language usage from including Native languages in worship songs (some languages had no tribal representatives present in the service, such as the use of Jonathan Maracle's Broken Walls songs, which are at least partially sung in Mohawk), only an offertory prayer spoken in Lakota (Eagle Butte Church of God, Eagle Butte, SD), an entire sermon preached in both English and Navajo (Window Rock Church of God, Window Rock, AZ), to an entire service with no Native language whatsoever (Cherokee Church of God, Cherokee, NC).

Kyle Taylor is a Pawnee and Choctaw from the Southern Plains. His use of dance, language, song, and regalia all reflect this cultural area. Language is one of the few contextualized traditional practices churches employ, and this, of course, strongly impacts their understanding since language shapes Native thinking about spiritual issues as they consider these ideas within the Church. James Murie was recommended to me in my interview with Taylor as someone who had written extensively on the Pawnee.[2] Taylor told me that Murie had translated a number of stories written by his grandfather, a Pawnee chief, that can be found in the 'Chicago Book Museum' (by which I believe he meant the University of Chicago library). It is my personal interview with Taylor that primarily informs the following analysis.

Critical Contextualization

My interview with Taylor led to a helpful discussion of language that gave insight into the points of common importance that both Christianity and Native American traditional religion share. The

---

[1] Kyle Taylor, 'Personal Interview', Muskogee, OK (2009).

[2] G.A. Dorsey and J.R. Murie, *Notes on Skidi Pawnee Society* (Whitefish, MT: Kessinger Publishing, 2006); A.C. Fletcher, J.R. Murie, and E.S. Tracy, *The Hako: A Pawnee Ceremony* (Washington, DC: Govt. Printing Office, 1904); J.R. Murie, *Pawnee Indian Societies* (New York: The Trustees, 1914); J.R. Murie and D.R. Parks, *Ceremonies of the Pawnee* (Washington, DC: Smithsonian Institution Press, 1981).

primary reason that no other interviews are utilized for this section on language is that Taylor was the only one who desired to talk about the subject.

I will follow the specific steps (phenomenological examination, testing beliefs, and so on) from Hiebert in this case but will engage them in a more general way in the remaining cases in order to allow the analysis to help modify Hiebert's approach to critical contextualization.

Phenomenological Examination

Taylor's phenomenological examination is internal, as he reflects on his own Native religion from a Christian perspective. This speeds up the process, as there is no need for a missionary to do the phenomenological inquiry. Taylor can do this work with authority because he is the descendant of a Pawnee chief and has reflected upon and researched his own Native beliefs.[3]

Testing Beliefs and Practices in Light of Biblical Truth and Tests of Reality

In the interview, it became clear to me that Taylor has reflected upon his own Pawnee and Choctaw culture to the extent that he can find evidence of a previous time when God dealt with his people before the Christian message reached their tribe. He finds this in the linguistic evidence of certain terms for God. He resolves this issue by citing Paul's sermon at the Areopagus in Acts 17. His biblical reflections reveal his deep commitment to biblical truth. His understanding of the cross can be seen in the songs and stories that he contextualizes, even down to the regalia he wears. He finds his contextualized Christianity to be his own reality, rather than the previous form of ministry he held in days past.[4]

Evaluating Old Beliefs and Practices in the Light of Biblical Truth

Taylor exercises spiritual discernment in the ways he speaks about certain traditions of the past that he rejects, such as polygamy. He says:

Syncretism is 'bringing pagan rituals mixed with godly worship'. Some traditions we don't do. Slavery wasn't good and polygamy

---

[3] Taylor, 'Personal Interview'.
[4] Taylor, 'Personal Interview'.

wasn't good. Those we do are held up to Scripture. Old Testament has to hold up to New Testament. Standards are very high. You can't let demonic stuff in the church. Sometimes in a worship service we stop and pray, asking God to clean out anything unpleasing to him.[5]

This quote refutes what a great many are saying in criticism of the contextual movement: that Native Americans use traditional practices uncritically. Taylor speaks critically of his past culture in regard to practices that the Bible would teach against, such as polygamy. He also cites his use of the Old and New Testaments in order to make discerning judgments. This is done prayerfully, according to Taylor, and demonic influence is watchfully prevented as this evaluation takes place. This speaks to the purpose of my study, demonstrating that non-Native denominational leaders have reason to trust many of the experienced Indian elders to carry out a thoughtful test of any traditional practices that would be brought into the worship service. I have witnessed this type of testing which was described in my interviews and observations.

Taylor performs an interesting Pentecostal hermeneutic as he speaks of language in his spiritual experience.[6] He states:

They've got my Great-Grandpa's painting in the Indian health plant because he was just such a great healer, they said. They honor him by putting that up; he painted himself black and he put white spots on himself. I have this silverware with this Morning Star symbol, which is a symbol of the Pawnees that my Great-Grandpa talks about, and I wear those when I dance. It's not just because, because I can worship my God with the contemporary style, I love to, I love to. It's kind of like, you can pray in your understanding and you can pray in tongues; its something different. And that for me, that's the difference, I can worship God, in another's man style and I can touch him, or I can worship him in the way that he created me to be.[7]

Taylor has a specific tribal tradition that he can point to and is not ashamed to wear proudly the symbols of his ancestors when he

---

[5] Taylor, 'Personal Interview'.

[6] Nowhere else have I heard an approach to language presented in this way.

[7] Taylor, 'Personal Interview'.

worships in a Christian way. He is also flexible in that he can move in different modes in his personal worship of Jesus. He, like many American Indians, is adept in moving in at least two worlds. When he does speak of changing modes in worship from contemporary to traditional Indian, he speaks of a Pentecostal paradigm. He compares his modal change to that of the Pentecostal worshiper moving from praying intelligibly to prayer in tongues as enabled by the Holy Spirit. This is significant for my study as my focus is Pentecostal churches that interpret their experiences in ways different from typical evangelicals.

Ministries that Transform Individuals and Congregations to Move from Where They Are to Where God Wants Them to Be

Taylor's ministry of evangelism extends to powwows, churches, and various other events, where he ministers for Christ. Teaching young people in the weekly classes at Bacone College is a joy for him, and he does this through both appreciating the songs and stories of his hereditary Pawnee culture as well as extending that teaching ministry in pastoral and prophetic fashion.

Language as Revelation of God

> In the beginning there was the Word, and the Word was with God, and the Word was God. And the Holy Spirit and the Word complement each other so powerfully. So I like how you can see all of those examples, some are Western perspective, and I think that with Indians, you have to go way back and you see things like the Grand Peace Policy and all of that and what it was meant to do. And one of the things that the government did is that they outlawed and forbade Indians from speaking their own language. For instance if you go back, there is this old song, it's incredible, and it talks about the Savior, and the Healer coming. And the inference from that song is 'get ready'. And it's a war dance song, the Savior and the Healer is coming. And if you talk to some of the older men, they talk about God; they talk about the Creator that he is coming. Well, when they outlawed that song and that language, it really created a little vacuum or a hole in Native people.[8]

---

[8] Taylor, 'Personal Interview'.

The loss of Native language, historically, has served to impoverish the faith of Native peoples, first because revelation comes (and often in a Pentecostal context) by verbal inspiration. This gives special significance to language in the worship context as something other than just the communication of ideas with a dynamic equivalence. The prohibition of Native language did far more damage than just to take away the memory of a bygone era. The tribal language carried cultural reality in more ways than just the conveyance of ideas. In the Native context, God not only reveals himself verbally as in John chapter one, but secondly, spirituality is imbedded in language.

Spirituality Imbedded in Language

> Even the words that you know, you couldn't mistake them for anything but something spiritual. For example, the Creeks, their word for God is … I can't even pronounce it, my wife can, but the word means 'the giver of breath'. But you couldn't even speak those words, because no one knew what they were. So consequently I think that the worldview, the spiritual worldview that was embedded in the language and came out, when people spoke or sang, or told stories. They never got past them; it was generations of gaps from these stories.[9]

Early missionaries to Native Americans may or may not have known this. Whether they helped to preserve Native language as a control mechanism to be able to translate Scripture and stay in control with how the people worshiped, or whether it was a genuine attempt to help the people is a historian's call. There were 'language churches' that spoke tribal languages.

Taylor believes that in order for a Pentecostal church to be truly contextual, the church has to be speaking in a local tribal language. He states, '… but I believe that language qualifies you as a contextual church'. He believes this because words create worldview.

Words Create Worldview

> So they got into those churches and everybody had to speak and sing in English, and as time went on, some of these churches began to be efforts, or models, or notions, or approaches. And

---

[9] Taylor, 'Personal Interview'.

they were trying to reach their people, but then noticed that they were not reaching anybody, small little churches. And they wondered what was going to create some energy and to allow them to get back and really reach the folks in the community who didn't know who the Lord was. So it was almost like if they rediscovered the language. And with the re-discovering of the language, they started really looking, and finding out what these words meant and things like that, and you know – learn from elders, and they realized that those words created a world-view that they had really gotten away from.[10]

Here Taylor expresses in his own words the longings and motivations that have resulted in the contextual movement's vision and missional desire. His description of the language used in churches reveals the degree of missionary failure in the policies of civilization and assimilation. His statements show the importance of language in the dual effect of being a window to culture as well as an indicator of God's previous involvement with a historic culture before the gospel formally came through the witness of missionaries.

Language and Scripture

The relationship of contextualizing traditional Native language and Scripture is imbedded more in the nature of the composition of the Bible than anything that the Bible specifically teaches. The critical school of thought approaches the original linguistic riches as carrying a great deal of revelatory power both in revealing the original cultures in which the Bible was written, but also in more fully revealing the God of the Bible in ways that one language, such as English, is insufficient to capture. This includes literary devices such as dual meanings and word pictures.

That's the same way as in the linguistically different words and different tribes; they have dual meanings just like when you translate the word 'power' – you know, you read it in the New Testament. In Luke, you know, it says; 'Behold, I give unto you power to tread on serpents and scorpions, and over all the power of the enemy: and nothing shall by any means hurt you'. Those two words 'power' in that verse, they are two different Greek words; and they mean two different things, and it's the

---

[10] Taylor, 'Personal Interview'.

same thing with the Indian languages you know, they have dual meanings, and you really have to look at them and understand. And a lot of languages are like the Hebrew, just like the Indians, they paint pictures. It's not just one word that can define that, just like the word 'water' for the Pawnee it means water, but it also means melted ice. So you know, when they were trying to come up with water and drinking, the Pawnee were there way back in the ice age and they saw the ice melting. So yeah, for instance there's a word that I mentioned the other day that means, 'you belong to me'. But really, the word that comes out of that is, 'I'll provide for you, or I care for you', so it has that dual meaning; so it just means that because we belong to him, he is going to take care of us. And when they translate that song, it talks about that meaning, and that message of him providing and always taking care of us. But the word really means 'belong, property of' and that kind of thing. Of course it's said in a positive way, not a negative one. So that's the notion, the definition that comes out of that word and it's interesting because there will be a lot of people who will talk about the Indian languages reminding them of Hebrew, because instead of going from left to right it goes from right to left. And it has dual meanings, and it's really hard to translate at times.[11]

There is a certain affinity that Native Americans have with Hebrew peoples that I will not fully examine in this study, but this quote from Taylor reveals one of the ways that Indians identify with the Hebrew tribes to whom God initially revealed himself through ritual.

Comparison
There is a deeper significance to the language that Taylor is referring to here. He is actually referring to an approach to Native language much like the linguistic approach that biblical scholars take toward Hebrew language. The idea is that it is of a Divine nature that yields a certain depth spiritually, even having layers of meaning. My reason for speaking of this is to underscore the fact that Native American culture is not disposable and that it even holds benefit as a realm in which God has been moving before the gospel was ever

---

[11] Taylor, 'Personal Interview'.

shared with Native peoples. For this reason, I am convinced that all non-Native censure should cease, and Native leadership should take charge of the decision-making process. The deeper significance given to language in this case of contextualization goes beyond any outsider's view of language as a conveyor of information or even a carrier of culture. Language contextualized in this way is in a sense, revelatory.

Taylor's contextualization appears to be deeper than what happens generally in the contextual movement, and the fact that he is a Pentecostal causes me to see his mode of contextualization as more meaningful. The problem is that the average Native American can have at least two tribes behind their name, and pure tribal traditions in many places have been mixed with inter-tribal practices.

Another approach, which Taylor does not consider to be true contextualization, is the carte-blanche usage of Indian language in inter-tribal worship services. This, according to Taylor, has to do with protocol.

> Well, I think there is a difference, because it doesn't mean that the Cherokee can't do a Pawnee dance. It doesn't mean that. But from a scholarly point of view there are those politics of recognition. There are those theoretical concerns and those reciprocal protocols and part of those politics of recognition is that you know, authenticity. So something that I like to talk about in my tribe is that the authenticity is that I have had an elder from my tribe give me affording approval to speak on those aspects of the culture.[12]

In my observations of contextual worship services, I would have to say that what Taylor is here calling for is quite difficult. The variety of tribal expression, the inclusion of non-Natives in their participation of the worship, and the relatively scattered nature of tribal peoples both urban and rural, makes this standard, in my view, almost impossible to maintain. What must be guarded against is the total disrespect for protocol that results from this impossibility.

Another case where language is contextualized in a different way than what Taylor is describing is the use of contextual Native praise songs and choruses. I heard songs by Jonathan Maracle (Mohawk)

---

[12] Taylor, 'Personal Interview'.

and Broken Walls in several of the churches that I visited, either played on CD or sung in worship and praise times. One description from my participant observation of Sacred Ground Outreach is in order here.

> The songs used were mostly RainSong and Broken Walls numbers, but soon Pastor Lundy described some songs as chants as 'cry of a heart'. The first song done was 'Yahweh' (glory, honor, power, and praise), the next one was 'Dance for the Rain', then 'Holy, Holy Spirit', 'Ah Nio'. Soon children were called up to the beautiful myrtle wood gathering drum, where they played the drum along with the adults in praise. There were about fifty people present. On the overhead was written 'Praise Jesus, our Creator, Savior, Healer, and Returning Chief' (Personal Observation notes 3/29/09).

It is exciting to me to see how Natives use Maracle's songs, which include the Mohawk language. This type of inter-tribal usage of language, ceremony and the like is common in the contextual movement. History bears out that from first contact Native Americans spoke at least some other trade languages with members of other tribes, so it is not unreasonable for Native churches to feature a variety of Native languages.

Transformed Practice
Exactly how Taylor contextualizes Native language can be seen in the way he treats ancient Pawnee stories and songs.

> We will contextualize some of the old traditional stories. My grandfather on my dad's side was the hereditary Pawnee chief, but he was also a deer doctor and also a scout. Later on in his life he became a believer, but he has a number of stories that are written in Pawnee mythology and books you can find in the Chicago Book Museum. But anyways, what I have done is I have taken those stories, traditional stories that were originally spoken in the Pawnee language, and translated them by an ethnologist of that time, James Murie.[13]

> So we take those stories and we look at them historically, and we look at the context in which they were told and also look at the

---

[13] See Murie, *Pawnee Indian Societies*.

morals of the story and then we contextualize those stories. One in particular, is one about the dance I told you about earlier. You know it's this ceremony or ritual that's from this war dance, you know, the eagle feather, the roach and the spreader, and so we get to come out and we get to talk to the students, talk to the staff or just anyone there, and then tell them things like, 'You are going to be an eagle', 'You are going to be a roach'.[14] 'But the good news is that there's going to be a bone spreader there that's going to hold you up'. And that spreader there used to be known by the Indians as war dancers in the 'her-ush-ka' style. But the power of that story is that, yes, you are going to go through all that stuff and all those roaches and what not, but the good news is that like in Proverbs it says that it's 'medicine to your flesh'. And health is translated to medicine, so we talk to them about the medicine that's a part of this story, and that medicine, we find out, it's God's Word that's going to help them.

So we have shared a lot of that with different tribes cause those stories can transfer if you go back and you tell them their original historical meaning. So what I major on is, like I said, regalia, dance, song, and story, because they are all tied together. Those songs are stories; they have vocals just like I told you. There is one song in particular that we sing a lot and the message it has is that it's him that is taking care of us, it's our Heavenly Father. Those are the words. That's not a contemporary song, that's an old-time song that, you know, like we didn't have churches, we had gatherings and they would sing that song. And at the end, the tale talks about thanking the Heavenly Father that he is going to take care of us and some of the words infer that we belong to him. And so the Pawnee wanted to teach their children, teach their young that we belong to him, that he is going to take care of us, and we are going to thank him too.

So those are the major things I like to look at, I like to look at the stories that come out of that song, and then the dance is connected to that, and that is Pawnee. There is no inter-

---

[14] In this context, a 'roach' is a name taken from the roached mane of a horse for a porcupine headdress (Powers, 'Native American Music of the Twentieth Century', p. 154).

tribalism, there is no Pan-Indianism in that, so those things are pure.[15]

Here Taylor gives us insight into the internal process of how a contextual Pentecostal preacher sees the powerful gift of pre-Christian revelation residing in the language. What is also a gift in Taylor's words is the information that is normally obscured by pro-tocol issues. Also to be seen is the strong role of language in con-textualization that works effectively as an evangelistic tool for him. Taylor does, however, have a somewhat exclusive view of language use in this case that he seems to feel is superior to any inter-tribal usage. Nowhere else in my interviews do my interviewees seem to denigrate the usage of the practices in inter-tribal contextual wor-ship.

My interviews and participant observations revealed two realities that are supported by Taylor's words. First, the interviews I con-ducted revealed a desire on the part of Native ministries to reach out and evangelize the tribal traditional people, using the tribal lan-guages they hold dear. In the participant observations of the wor-ship services, it took the form of announcements in which out-reaches were planned to certain reservations where distinctly Native presentations would be given. In each case, there is special signifi-cance attached to gospel presentations given by Indians, for Indi-ans.

Smudging

Then, what looked like flames or tongues of fire appeared and settled on each of them (Acts 2.3).

Smudging may be the most controversial traditional practice I ob-served being contextualized in the Native American Pentecostal churches. This is surprising due to the clear presence of incense in Scripture and the historic use of it in traditions such as the Roman Catholic and Eastern Orthodox Churches.

Practice Description
The smudge is a cleansing or purification ceremony that cleanses body, soul, and spirit. It is done by lighting sage, sweet grass, or

---

[15] Taylor, 'Personal Interview'.

cedar, and then blowing out the fire causing it to smoke in a shell. In order to obtain cleansing, the Native person pulls the smoke onto them while the one burning the sage waves an eagle feather or fan to move the smoke. The smell of the sage, sweet grass, or cedar is a beautiful scent.

> We will get a container with the burning sage, generally a sea shell or some other traditional container that Native people use. The minister will hold it in his right hand and you will have a feather in the left hand, and you know, brush the smoke onto the person, and that takes the place as you say, the anointing with oil [as is done in other churches]. As oil is not the Holy Spirit, but a symbol of the Holy Spirit, the smudging ceremony is kind of a touch point, symbolic of the Holy Spirit.[16]

Critical Contextualization

Barnetson identified smudging as a pan-Indian practice.[17] The interview that took place late one night, while Barnetson was driving his family back home to the Los Angeles area, after attending a family camp and contextual powwow, focused on several First Nations topics. Barnetson freely talked about smudging, which is clearly important in his church services. He dealt with smudging in detail, predictably, based upon my previous talk with him. For Barnetson, contextualization

> has the effect of actually just making people understand the spiritual truth by using a Native activity and attributing new and expanded and deeper meaning to it, and people interpreting that we embrace their culture, you see, you know that there's some value to what they do and that their customs are not though unworthy and to be thrown out, but actually can be used to illustrate spiritual truth.[18]

In my nine interviews, smudging was discussed in almost all the conversations. The interviewees had a basis upon which to argue for its legitimacy from culture and Scripture. I witnessed it being done in only four out of my nine participant observations. The rea-

---

[16] Randy Barnetson, 'Telephone Interview with Randy Barnetson', Santa Fe Springs, CA (2007).

[17] Barnetson, 'Telephone Interview with Randy Barnetson'.

[18] Barnetson, 'Telephone Interview with Randy Barnetson'.

son for this, I believe, is due to the controversial nature of the practice and possibly something as simple as the sensitivity of smoke alarms. Barnetson's reference to smudging as a vehicle to teach spiritual truth is a good example of redemptive analogy used in a Native context. This idea will be described in more detail later in the study.

As in Hiebert's model, it is clear that phenomenological examination is being done, in an internal way, by First Nations believers. The Barnetsons are actively testing these beliefs and practices in light of biblical truth, as they study Scripture and minister in churches. Smudging is a cultural reality that Bear-Barnetson has known her whole life, and according to her words, her grandmother also contextualized smudging in her Christian experience.

Smudging is explained in light of and distinct from the redemptive work of Jesus Christ and held out in a sacramental way, emphasizing the symbol of an experience that is deeply spiritual. Discerning decision-making is an important part of their integration of practices, and they 'evaluate old beliefs and practices in the light of biblical truth' as they choose smudging as one practice to include, stemming from a distinctively Pentecostal hermeneutic based upon Mal. 1.11, in which God speaks positively of sincere people outside the community of faith offering incense in times past. Individuals are transformed as the transformed practice draws them into meaningful worship, embracing their appreciated culture.

The traditional belief is that the burning of sage carries cleansing powers, but First Nation people tend to use it in a symbolic manner. It traditionally was used to accompany prayer. Barnetson says, 'We will do the smudging, but in a symbolic manner. To say that it's symbolic is to say it doesn't have a power in and of itself. So we incorporate the ceremony of smudging'. Barnetson went on to explain how his congregation incorporates the practice of smudging:

> We have the typical evangelical ritual of communion and baptism … Along with baptism we incorporate smudging as well, now, as part of the baptismal experience. To Native people, the lighting of sage smoke, and using that smoke, the person will take smoke in their hands and kind of brush it on themselves, wash it over themselves, and they do that as being a cleansing ceremony, that they are actually cleansed of bad things or sin, or whatever; but in the church we'll use it symbolically. You know,

tell the people that it's not actually smoke that cleanses you, it's only a symbol, the same way that the waters of immersion baptism don't actually cleanse or wash away your sins, but it's symbolic. It's only an outward sign of an inward experience; the true cleansing took place by the blood of Jesus, you know, on the cross, when we accept it by faith.[19]

The Native American traditions place great emphasis on cleansing, so it follows that in a church where Native people worship, there should be a cleansing ceremony. Barnetson explains,

> Every single service we have smudging and cleansing ceremonies. To the Western mind it may be kind of an overkill, but to the Native mind it is something that they would do normally all the time to reinforce that teaching. It is very appropriate in the Native setting to have a lot of smudging taking place as part of the worship experience.[20]

The critical contextualization that Barnetson does here leads him to a sacramental approach to the practice with an argument that any evangelical would be familiar with regarding the 'outward sign of an inward experience'. This underscores what I found in general in both my interviews and observations. This is all something more than effect or style. There is a substantive significance to these practices in which Christian grace is being conferred. A deeper study might glean a similar theological significance that incense holds for some, such as Orthodox Christians.

Smudging and Scripture
The burning of incense is a practice found in the Old Testament and in the Eastern Tradition. Barnetson explains this by citing Mal. 1.10-12.

> How I wish one of you would shut the Temple doors so that these worthless sacrifices could not be offered! I am not pleased with you', says the Lord of Heaven's Armies, 'and I will not accept your offerings. But my name is honored by people of other nations from morning till night. All around the world they offer sweet incense and pure offerings in honor of my name. For my

---

[19] Barnetson, 'Telephone Interview with Randy Barnetson'.
[20] Barnetson, 'Telephone Interview with Randy Barnetson'.

name is great among the nations', says the Lord of Heaven's Armies.

Before Christ, Natives see their people as offering 'an anointing with fire'. Another ritual that is common in the Pentecostal Charismatic tradition is also related to the Barnetsons' contextualized practice of smudging: anointing. Barnetson refers to the James 5 passage: 'Is any one of you sick? He should call the elders of the church to pray over him and anoint him with oil in the name of the Lord. And the prayer offered in faith will make the sick person well; the Lord will raise him up. If he has sinned, he will be forgiven' (Jas 5.14-15, NIV). Here the anointing with oil is to accompany prayer for the sick. Barnetson says,

> We see the oil, but here again, we will use the smudging again, which is very much appreciated in the Native church, so we'll use the smudging to also incorporate that concept that you have in other Pentecostal traditions where you are anointing people with oil for various things ... [I]nstead of anointing with oil, we will smudge.[21]

In Larry 'Grizz' Brown's discussion of smudging, he is evaluating old beliefs and practices in the light of biblical truth as he refers to Revelation where the smoke that goes up are the prayers of the saints. 'Smudging is the declaration of our need for cleansing'. The smoke is 'a visual representation of our need for cleansing'. In reference to the use of an eagle wing fan, it is representative to Isa. 40.31. He sums up the effect of contextual worship in this way: 'All our contextual efforts and deliberate worship ways in the context of our Native-ness just further emphasizes our devotion to the Lord and the freedom we have in him. This freedom that we have in him just intensifies my intimacy with him'.[22]

Comparison

Just as oil is a biblical symbol for the Holy Spirit, like wind, so is fire, and they use the sage smoke as a way to incorporate the symbolism for the fire of the Holy Spirit. Barnetson contends, 'That's what the burning sage and smoke is – it's fire. So practically what's

---

[21] Barnetson, 'Telephone Interview with Randy Barnetson'.

[22] Larry 'Grizz' Brown, 'Telephone Interview with Larry "Grizz" Brown', Apple Valley, CA (2007).

happening is we are smudging the person; but theologically we explain that they are being *anointed with fire'* (emphasis added). Here again, Barnetson likes to refer to 'a new and expanded meaning', a fitting description of contextualization or transformation.[23] Every time Barnetson and his congregation practice smudging, they explain the symbolism. Barnetson sees doing this as similar to what Don Richardson spoke about in *Peace Child*.[24] Barnetson says, 'There's something within the culture, and he uses that to illustrate Christ'.[25] Natives would not necessarily associate fire with healing, so this is an example of a Pentecostal transformation or, in Barnetson's terms, the 'adding and expanding' of the traditional smudging practice.

Transformed Practice
The levels that I perceive Barnetson is describing could be summed up this way: There is an affirming and 'welcoming effect' in featuring smudging in a Pentecostal worship service for Native people. Beyond that, there is an understanding that smudging holds a cleansing function for all those that come forward. Thirdly, there is, through the added and expanded meaning, a Pentecostal 'anointing with fire', and an opportunity to allow the worshiper to be introduced to and be touched by the Holy Spirit in this beautifully contextualized practice. I had this done to me and benefited greatly from it. While the Barnetsons are not the first or the only Natives to contextualize smudging, they are very instrumental in the spreading of this practice.

Other practices which Barnetson identified as important and suitable for contextualization were 'good speaking', dancing as prayer,[26] and the use of indigenous instruments. Barnetson simply describes Native American contextualization as a move to 'embrace the practice, expand the meaning and allow the Natives to be gently brought along'.[27]

There are cases where smudging is used in conjunction with tobacco (not in my observations of Pentecostal churches), but in those cases, a Pentecostal understanding is applied to the practice:

---

[23] Barnetson, 'Telephone Interview with Randy Barnetson'.
[24] Richardson, *Peace Child*.
[25] Barnetson, 'Telephone Interview with Randy Barnetson'.
[26] Twiss, *Dancing Our Prayers*.
[27] Barnetson, 'Telephone Interview with Randy Barnetson'.

Let me just say this about smudging; the Pawnee believe that the cedar tree represents God because that cedar tree never dies, it's always alive. And so you have tobacco, and it's cedar, and the Pawnee believe that that's the breath of God. My grandpa would take people's prayers and blow them in the tobacco or the cedar, and blowing it, and then you know, the way that they would grab it out of the air, pat them down and smudge them because they were taking people's prayers with them – and you know they may have been walking by faith and maybe not as much as people are today – and they would smell that and it would help him remember the prayers that people had offered for them; and then I knew that it was going to be a success. They didn't think that they would be overcomers because it was taking their prayers with him. The smudging is praying you know, it's like I said – you can pray, but when you use tobacco, cedar, sage, sweet grass, that's like praying in tongues. People can pray in their own languages, and they are still praying in their under-standing; but when they got that tobacco and cedar and sage out, and they will send represented aspects of life to them. That's like praying in their tongues; they believe that they were grabbing a hold of, capturing God. And it took faith to do those things, and great things happened when they prayed like that.[28]

In the examples of smudging, it can be seen that in the contextual movement smudging has a variety of usages from symbolic to deeply transformational. Barnetson sees it as a symbolic 'fire anointing', with certain spiritual benefits, but primarily symbolic. Taylor describes a deeper transformational experience likened to speaking in tongues, which carries deep significance for Pentecostals. He sees it as an intensifying experience of taking hold of God in worship. Taylor stands out as an exception in my findings as a Pentecostal who allows for tobacco usage, or admits to doing so.

Drums and Rattles

Suddenly, there was a sound from heaven like the roaring of a mighty wind-storm, and it filled the house where they were sitting (Acts 2.2, NLT).

---

[28] Taylor, 'Personal Interview'.

The use of drums and rattles is, in general, the practice with the longest sustained rejection in churches worldwide. This is due to the ongoing suspicion that Euro-Americans have of the spiritual significance of drums in tribal practice. In spite of this widespread rejection of drums and rattles, I observed their use in almost every group in my study.

Practice Description

Bear-Barnetson says that the 'big drum' was present at one of the first important gatherings of Foursquare Natives.

> So all of the Native leaders of America got together – and I think that it was first in Denver – and so we were invited to that because we were the only Native pastors in Foursquare Canada at least. So we were really thrilled to be part of that. And so then we met again, and the point of those meetings were that we all felt like there was a need to stop and develop a nationality and recognize national ministry to Native people that was distinct from multi-cultural and distinct from a geographical unit ... So to us, we need someone who is not geographical, that can bring First Nations people together and build up the identity and use cultural aspects, so at the very first meeting we had a big drum.[29]

The 'big drum', according to Bear-Barnetson, is an inter-tribal cultural symbol that serves to unite Native Americans. In this aspect, it is especially important as a calling together of Native people, and then an important praise instrument for inviting the presence of God's Spirit into the worship and interactions of the people. Though not all of the services I observed included it, those that did gave it great attention by beginning the service with it.

Critical Contextualization

Pastor Larry 'Grizz' Brown, a Southeastern Creek/Cherokee pastor serving in California, distinguishes his drum team from traditional ones:

> We are not a powwow drum, we are not a traditional drum, we are a worship drum. It is a new tradition among born again Native people who walk in the freedom of worshiping God with

---

[29] Cheryl Bear-Barnetson, 'Cheryl Bear Barnetson Interview', Vancouver, BC (2008).

the beauty of our dance and song and actions. It is a new tradition, and I hope one day it will be an old tradition. I do not have the experience of powwow drum protocol.[30]

Brown distinguishes between a powwow drum, a traditional drum, and a worship drum. In doing so, he points to the different approaches to the traditional instruments. This was clear in my observational experience. I saw not just the inclusion of a powwow drum in a Native worship service; but I observed that the prayer that began over the drum was a different prayer, the songs were different, and the attitude was different.

Next, Brown talks about the hand drum, which he also played with skill at the Azusa Street Gathering.

The hand drum is a very personal drum. It's very easy to carry around and very easy to keep close at hand. It needs to be kept, and when you put it away, it needs to be treated with respect and cared for respectfully so whenever you take it out of its wrapping, its covering, other onlookers will know that you respect that drum as much as you do the big one. It is held and played by one person, and often three or four or more of us will gather with hand drums and do some very similar songs; and each drum has its own individual tone. All the sounds together form a beautiful chord that begins to resonate, and I have never heard that with anything but hand drums. The drums themselves begin to sing.

The use of hand drum is particularly significant for Brown, who has a story to tell about how his wife was transformed while playing one.

They passed out 120 hand drums, and one was handed to my wife. And as she was adding her worship and the beat on the drum given to her, there was a transformation that came over her. It was when she was drumming, I believe, that the Lord gave her a very clear vision of not only what he had called me to, but what he had called us to. It was when she played the

---

[30] Brown, 'Telephone Interview with Larry "Grizz" Brown'.

drum that it got into her spirit the understanding of what was going on.[31]

This comment demonstrates that the drumming is a ministry that transforms individuals to move them from where they are to where God wants them to be. Larry Brown's church, Living Way Foursquare Church, utilizes the following traditional practices: worship drum, hand drum, rattles, rain stick, bells on regalia, dance, smudging, burning sage, sweet grass and cedar. They do not burn tobacco, and they do not include talking circles at this time.

In terms of the connection between this Native American instrumental worship and his personal tribe of origin, Pastor Brown points out that among the over 500 tribes there are 'hundreds of ways of doing the same thing' and that the questions that are asked about contextualization might elicit any number of legitimate answers from the various tribes. But he says,

> My ancestors made the agonizing choice to stay on the land of their ancestors, and honor that land, even though there was a law … written in Georgia at that time that said no Indian people in the State of Georgia. If they were found, they would be captured, arrested, and in most cases hanged. So a lot of the Indians stopped being Indian by culture. So I believe that the Lord Jesus by his Holy Spirit has given me a big heart for all of my people who were told that it was bad to be Indian, 'You can't do it!' And by all means, 'You cannot worship in this Native pagan way'. When the Lord gave this freedom to me, I feel like I carry in my spirit-being the weight of declaring for all my ancestors that we are who we are. God made us to be who he made us to be, and he did not make any mistakes.[32]

At this point, Brown begins to detail from Acts 17 the origin of the tribes, which Barnetson later explains. This is a common explanation among this larger group. Later in the interview Brown describes smudging with the same Scripture passages as Barnetson would later use. When asked, 'How do you feel when you worship the Creator in the Indian way?', he explained,

---

[31] Brown, 'Telephone Interview with Larry "Grizz" Brown'.
[32] Brown, 'Telephone Interview with Larry "Grizz" Brown'.

We come before the Lord, blessed and honored that we can sit down at an instrument made of wood and hide and worship him with a drum that has been made by the hands of men from the things that were made by the hands of God. And when we dance, every flutter of a feather, every sway of a fringe is a praise, an act of worship. Every time our foot touches the ground or the floor, it is a cry out to God, a prayer for the healing of our nation, and our nations within this nation. So it's a very physical, very purposeful act of worship. When I come before the Lord, I consider my eagle feathers, my regalia, my beadwork, the many different bracelets, necklaces, other things that have been given, I consider them to be my priestly garment, and I wear these garments not only when I worship, but I wear them when I serve. When I am ministering with the laying on of hands, or when I am ministering in the prophetic realm, or ministering forth the Word of God, in my own way, I guess I feel like a Levite, called and appointed, set apart to serve in the house of God. When we come to that drum, all these things that are part of our daily life, our daily challenges and daily pressures, we just bring it all before the Lord and we just offer it up to him in worship and praise, and we do it like nobody's looking.[33]

This is Brown's reality as he tests his beliefs in the light of biblical truth.

Drums, Rattles, and Scripture

Brown began his interview by launching right in to a biblical explanation of instrumental praise from the Psalms, first by citing the 'new song', which the title he has given to this fresh practice of praise in the contextual movement.

Praise the Lord! Praise God in his sanctuary; praise him in his mighty heaven! Praise him for his mighty works; praise his unequaled greatness! Praise him with a blast of the ram's horn; praise him with the lyre and harp! Praise him with the tambourine and dancing; praise him with strings and flutes! Praise him with a clash of cymbals; praise him with loud clanging cymbals. Let everything that breathes sing praises to the Lord! Praise the Lord! (Ps. 150.1-6)

---

[33] Brown, 'Telephone Interview with Larry "Grizz" Brown'.

Brown cites Psalm 150 from the New Living Translation and points out the use of the tambourine, but goes to the King James Version to identify the tambourine as a timbrel.

> A timbrel was a type of a tambourine without the little cymbals on it. It was basically a hand drum. So we are given instructions to praise the Lord with timbrels. Moses' sister Miriam, when they crossed the Red Sea, composed a song on the spot by dancing before the Lord, and sang a new song to him, playing a tambourine. They were made of wood, with the skin of an animal over it, probably a goatskin. Those were animals that were familiar to them. Our familiar animals are deer, elk, buffalo, and horse and in later years, even cow for drumheads. So the Word of God doesn't tell us not to play our Native instruments, it tells us to play our Native instruments.[34]

What is going on in Brown's discussion was also evident in Taylor's discussion. There is a biblical and Jewish basis for the inclusion of Native traditional instruments in worship. Brown, like Taylor, appeals to Hebrew word studies to make the vital connection. This was fascinating for me to observe, and I would suggest that it represents what is truly a transformed practice.

The flute emerges also in Brown's exegesis of Psalm 150, as indicated by the verse that says, 'Praise him with strings and flutes'. 'We play a lot of flutes', says Brown,[35] and it was evident from my participant observations that flutes are a strong presence in these Native American services. Brown refers to praise in very Pentecostal ways by saying, 'Worship should make a lot of noise, and it should rattle the community'.[36] At this point, he begins to talk about the drum, which I expected him to do. His drum team, Rainshadow, uses an old earth tone, hollowed out, cottonwood log, covered with animal hide. Brown describes the drum team experience: 'Every beat of that drum is a cry from my heart of gratitude for his work on the cross. I am personally worshiping when I am at that drum, and all those who join with me at that drum are the

---

[34] Brown, 'Telephone Interview with Larry "Grizz" Brown'.
[35] Brown, 'Telephone Interview with Larry "Grizz" Brown'.
[36] Brown, 'Telephone Interview with Larry "Grizz" Brown'.

same way'. At another point, Brown said, 'We know that the Lord God gave us this instrument'.[37]

Comparison

Contextualizers sometimes vary from the traditional approach to the drum, and in so doing, remove the fear of syncretism regarding it. First, in the contexts I observed, the drum appears to be constructed by believers who are spiritually sensitive. This makes the issues of spirit less threatening and reduces syncretism. In one drum that Dan Lundy (Rogue River) uses, the drum is beautifully constructed of myrtle wood, native to the area, which reminds the worshipers of the spatial dimension of their worship and the sacredness of the land on which they are praising the Creator. Also Lundy points out that olive oil was used in the treatment of the myrtle wood, which points to the Christian dimension of their spiritual identity, as well as the anointing of the Holy Spirit that they anticipate to accompany their times of worship of the true and living God. This is a contextualization of what would normally be a very traditional act.

Lundy's drum, used at Sacred Ground Outreach, was actually lined on the inside with handwritten Scriptures before the skin was adhered, obscuring their view. This is a powerful statement by the Church toward the traditional view of the drum having a heart and is a theological statement of the church's belief concerning the sacred nature of Holy Scripture. I have already spoken about the significance of drum decoration in the traditional American Indian context, so this is a vivid example of Native American contextualization.[38]

Transformed Practice

What was significant in my interview with Brown (Creek/Cherokee), and what stood out to me, was a threefold stage of traditional development. This coincided with what Barnetson spoke of in terms of smudging. Brown speaks of a 'traditional drum', a 'pow-wow drum', and a 'worship drum'. It appears that the three historical periods in Native American musical performance can be used as an outline to lead Natives from traditional practice into Pentecostal worship. This transformed usage of the Native gathering drum has

---

[37] Brown, 'Telephone Interview with Larry "Grizz" Brown'.
[38] Dan Lundy, 'Interview', Siletz (2009).

evolved into a very profound instrument in the ministry of Pentecostal praise.

Dance

Let them praise his name in the dance: let them sing praises unto him with the timbrel and harp (Ps. 149.3 KJV).

Native dance is contextualized more easily in the Pentecostal context due to the precedent of dancing in the Pentecostal-Charismatic tradition. Native American dance holds tremendous spiritual significance in the traditional context.

Practice Description

The dances performed in the Pentecostal worship services I observed were partly spontaneous and partly based on steps that had been learned, many of which were typical powwow dances. They included Northern Traditional, War Dance, and others.[39] Pentecostal Natives believe that dancing is scriptural, and they dance with confidence. Many of the dances have their origin in specific tribes, but only retain specific relationships to them, and become a part of the larger powwow inter-tribal selections.[40] The contextual movement features both social and ceremonial powwow dancing in the services that are contextualized in the practice of spiritual dancing in the Pentecostal tradition. That is, dancing before the Lord is both expressive worship and personally transformational and can be spontaneous or based on learned dances.[41]

Critical Contextualization

Certain aspects of traditional Native American dance do not immediately fit in a Christian context, so that a contextual approach is necessary to make the proper expressions. In this case, we might be witnessing a degree of 'Christological impasse',[42] or merely a Euro-American culture clash with Native dance:

---

[39] Taylor, 'Personal Interview'.

[40] Taylor, 'Personal Interview'; Bear-Barnetson, 'Cheryl Bear Barnetson Interview'.

[41] Taylor, 'Personal Interview'.

[42] Yong, *Discerning the Spirit(s)*, p. 33.

And so all the kinds of dances are just beautiful expressions of dancing; and so why not, why shouldn't it be allowed in the church or welcomed into the church? Because it is something that Natives love to do and it is also a cultural thing, you know. There are some songs that we sing where we bow down or we bow down before the Lord, and to Native people, there's nothing in their culture that talks about bowing. It is very much a biblical idea but it also it is something in a monarchial style of bowing down to the king or the queen, or whatever, you know. So Native people don't have a real concept of bowing before someone; there's a recognition of a leader between the group, [and] it is considered that one is the same as everyone [else]. So instead of one of the elders talking about bowing they talk about raising our hands to the heavens and praising the Lord.[43]

There are definite problems with European culture in its confrontation with Native Americans.[44] Bear-Barnetson gives an example here in dancing, that follows into other areas of Native American thought. Suffice it to say, dance is a practice that expresses a worship that in some ways confronts Euro-American culture. Nevertheless, a contextual Native American dance is a way of honoring the traditions of their people, and can be contextualized for Pentecostal worship.

Dancing and Scripture
As the Psalm quoted reminds us, there are exhortations throughout Scripture to dance before the Lord. As Pentecostals have done for decades, Native Pentecostals see no real problem in dancing in worship services. This may be the most easily contextualized practice in Native Pentecostal churches. Because there is a specific scriptural precedent, it raises less criticism.

Comparison
American Indians believe that they have an affinity with Jewish people, in that they break out into dance spontaneously with joy.

And so any sort of dance is seen in the Bible as a form of praise and a form of joy before the Lord; whenever there is a victory or

---

[43] Bear-Barnetson, 'Cheryl Bear Barnetson Interview'.
[44] The European concept of a monarch, or lord, is problematic for Native Americans, and extends even to the New Testament usage of 'Lord'.

souls have been won, people just break out into a dance. That might be a very cultural thing, like for Jewish people for them to dance, you know, like … Have you seen 'Fiddler on the Roof'? I'm not sure if that's a great example, but you know in the part where the guy just gets so happy that he starts to dance, and you sort of see that in celebratory times. I've seen that in different settings, you know like in Jewish and Greek settings in a wedding or at a feast, they will just break out into a dance. And I think that it is pretty much the same with Native people. I'm not sure about how that relates to Western culture, because it's not a cultural thing to break out into a traditional kind of dance in any part of the U.S. You know we have dances like before a wedding, but its different, it's just not the same.[45]

Once again, as with Taylor and Brown, affinity with Hebrew culture is observed as a way to differentiate Indian worship from that which is Euro-American. It is vital to understand this aspect of Native practice and attitude to order to understand how Native practices express Native worldview. It is a distinctly different experience culturally, and in some ways spiritually. I have witnessed this in my observations, and it demonstrates the viability of my call for Native leadership in decision-making in contextual matters.

Transformed Practice

Most contextualized Native Americans, as well as many traditional Native Americans, believe that dancing is prayer.[46] In some cases, every step is regarded as a separate prayer.[47] The background for such a belief may be based on testimonies and traditions such as the 'Jingle Dress Dance':

What was happening was that a young girl was really sick. And so her dad had a dream that if she wore the certain style of dress … it has like little cones that when it shakes it has a bell-like sound. And so the dream tells him that if she wears that dress and dances, she will be healed. And so he made her this dress, and she danced and she was healed. So the Jingle Bell dance has become a dance of healing. And so that story has been passed

---

[45] Bear-Barnetson, 'Cheryl Bear Barnetson Interview'.
[46] Barnetson, 'Telephone Interview with Randy Barnetson'; Twiss, *Dancing Our Prayers*.
[47] Bear-Barnetson, 'Cheryl Bear Barnetson Interview'.

down not only from Native to Native but Christians too. But the origins of that song are also known in the non-Christian Native world. And that is a dance that was given by the Creator for healing, so why not have that in the church?[48]

So we see that even the traditional origin of certain dances find their meanings in the context of blessings like healing, which fit very well in the Pentecostal setting. The traditional significance of dancing is easily contexualized in the Native Pentecostal context, due to the fact that dancing in Native culture already has at its heart prayer and spirituality.

Talking Circles

They devoted themselves to the apostles' teaching and to the fellowship, to the breaking of bread and to prayer (Acts 2.42, NIV).

Talking circles, a place where the 'good speaking' of Native American interchanges takes place, both illustrates the powerful circle as a universal Native symbol and demonstrates the consensual nature of Native leadership. In the Native American contextual world, this circle has taken on expanded characteristics and has developed into something akin to the cell group or Christian support group, integrated with authentic Native spirituality.

Practice Description

The talking circle is led by a spiritual person, who passes around an eagle feather or talking stick to members of the circle. The participants take turns expressing their feelings or testimonies, whatever the case might be. The leader facilitates the discussion and deals with issues as they come forth. The healing effects of small group dynamics, coupled with affirmation and self-disclosure, are applied in the lives of all who follow the model in sincerity. When asked about the talking circles, Pastor Lundy referred to some talking circles as 'fire circles'. This reminds me of the 'anointing by fire' in Barnetson's smudging.[49] The fire circle not only connects with the 'tribal fire' in Native American culture, but actually refers to the circle being held around a bonfire and a written list of bondages or

---

[48] Bear-Barnetson, 'Cheryl Bear Barnetson Interview'.
[49] Lundy, 'Interview'.

sins thrown in to symbolize the cleansing and healing that Christ has brought the individual. This has direct connection with the Encounter Retreat in the G12 Movement, and other retreats that also involve the burning of profiles. The practice of contextualized Native American talking circles has been under-appreciated in the church context, probably due to its widespread use in New Age contexts. There is, however, a wonderful and rich resource for pastoral healing and community in this age-old practice of Native peoples.

Barnetson (First Nations, Santa Fe Springs) takes charge of the service at this point, passing a feather around to each worshiper, giving invitation for a word, testimony, prophecy, or song in the talking circle. Those who share use it either as a prayer request time, Bible class, sharing group, or support group. It is a moving experience. Some pass by, giving the feather to their neighbor, choosing not to share. One brother shares from Psalm 112, that our 'children will be mighty in the land'. Another Native man, Mark, shares how he is thankful that his son, with whom he went fishing earlier in the day, is now not only a fisher of men, but a drummer boy, praising his son's presence on the drum team. He also testifies of a new teaching job he has gotten teaching third graders in a charter school in Canoga Park.

When asked about the talking circles, Pastor Lundy, at Siletz Community Center, said:

> It is a small discussion group. Sometimes there is teaching on traumas and 'fire circles' are utilized. When someone has gone through a great healing, has confessed and repented and been refilled with the Holy Spirit, they build a fire in the middle of a circle outside. The more cultural things that are utilized are better.[50]

In my participant observation of the talking circle at the Barnetsons' church in Santa Fe Springs, it felt very much like the support groups I held for so many years. There was a dimension of affirmation that was unique and positive, which Barnetson later referred to as 'good speaking'. There is a great deal yet to be done in the study of this practice and its correlation to cell group methods.

---

[50] Lundy, 'Interview'.

Critical Contextualization

Being possibly the most easily contextualized Native American traditional practice I have witnessed yet, this small group model is very relevant to practices that are going on in many Pentecostal churches today. The internal phenomenological examination takes place in most all Native tribal cultures, and the talking circle may be the most universal of all these practices. Native pastors like Lundy and Barnetson are actually testing beliefs and practices in light of biblical truth and tests of reality in these very circles. This happens due to the communal nature of these gatherings, and they are transformed with the addition of Pentecostal testimony and group therapy methods. Brown exercises his own personal spiritual discernment by electing not to practice talking circles at this time.[51]

Talking circles are an example of healing ministries that transform individuals and move them from where they are to where God wants them to be. Lundy shares the evangelistic benefit as he ministers to the veteran who suffers from PTSD and uses the talking circle for teaching and pastoral functions.[52]

Talking Circles and Scripture

Native Americans apparently consider it unnecessary to point out a biblical basis for the talking circle, as it is an accepted practice in most Pentecostal, as well as evangelical, contexts. Baby Boomers are comfortable with the practice, as they have matured with the self-help movement's support group model being a constant reality in both social and medical practices. As I will point out in my section on ceremony, I conclude that the Native American community holds a key to many ills of our culture as they have an ancient experience in serving the needs of individuals who suffer from wartime injury. Due to the wide variety of preparation for and healing from war, ceremonies in the American Indian traditions have a rich contribution to make to a war-torn world.

Comparison

The talking circle used in Native American health-related and clinical settings and the talking circle I participated in at the First Nations Church may be compared to the combination of a community support group and a Pentecostal/Charismatic prayer, sharing, and

---

[51] Brown, 'Telephone Interview with Larry "Grizz" Brown'.
[52] Lundy, 'Interview'.

testimony group. The primary difference is that the Native American context has a distinct spirituality, whether the group is health-related or Christian in orientation. The Pentecostal version that I am studying normally incorporates testimony as an important feature. This was true of the talking circle that I attended.

Transformed Practice

The importance and use of talking circles in Native American life makes a natural blend with Pentecostal church life. It not only makes Native American culture easy to contextualize into Pentecostal practice and vice versa, but small groups are an important dimension of Pentecostal church growth at this particular time in history. The powerful American Indian Contextual Movement is poised to make an important impact at this juncture in Pentecostal history.

The Enemy Way Ceremony

> *Everyone was filled with awe, and many wonders and miraculous signs were done by the apostles. All the believers were together and had everything in common. Selling their possessions and goods, they gave to anyone as he had need. Every day they continued to meet together in the temple courts. They broke bread in their homes and ate together with glad and sincere hearts, praising God and enjoying the favor of all the people. And the Lord added to their number daily those who were being saved* (Acts 2.43-47, NIV).

Native American Pentecostals not only contextualize individual musical activities or isolated rituals, but entire traditional ceremonies have been transformed and sanctified for worship of Christ. The Enemy Way Ceremony, if embraced contextually, holds a key for important Christian healing to the sufferers of post-traumatic stress disorder.

Practice Description

The ceremony that I include and analyze here is one that represents a contextualized practice that could be regarded as more communal in nature in that it includes an entire community, not just participants of an individual worship service. The Navajo Enemy Way Ceremony is a healing ceremony that exists to minister to individuals. Conducted in the summer months, the ceremony is an almost week-long process for individuals who suffer from various forms of illness. It was originally conducted for warriors returning from war. This is the primary reason it was named the Nidaa', the Enemy Way Ceremony. Some people call it a 'squaw dance', but that is a derogatory name for what is a wonderful ceremony for the people. Appendix A contains the traditional version described by a traditional medicine man. Appendix B contains a complete description of how the contextualized version was carried out.

A young student suggested a contextualized Navajo Enemy Way Ceremony to me. He came to my wife's office, having heard about my research. He was a tall Navajo man who told me, 'You need to talk to my pastor'. My futile attempts to discover contextualized practices in my own Pentecostal denomination were about to be rewarded. This was not a ceremony that was an ongoing contextualized example, as were the others I had witnessed. This one was performed a number of times until the 1980s when denominational officials and local churches had denounced it as syncretistic. Some opponents even utilized the local newspaper (the Gallup, New Mexico *Independent*) to challenge the practice. This painful experience and the sincerity that the young student described to me touched my heart, and I became determined to honor this recent historical example that was still precious in the collective memory of the church, and which had such a powerful evangelistic effect, even beyond any subsequent event in the life of this local congregation.

I was not surprised to find that the church had been connected with the Foursquare Church in some type of relationship close to the time of the contextualized ceremony. I made the trip with my team to Window Rock, Arizona, and the famous 'Four Corners' of the Navajo Nation, located in the Native American cultural area known as the Southwest. This area of Arizona and New Mexico represents the largest Native American membership in my denomination, Church of God (Cleveland, TN).

The Enemy Way Ceremony is a ceremony that relates to war, as do many Native ceremonies and rituals. It is a communal celebration in which the sufferer who returns from battle emotionally wounded receives healing through a process of spiritual prayer and support. It traditionally involves the medicine man as well as the entire community.

My data for this practice is contained in Dennison's archival newspaper description (see Appendix A) and in the recollections of the Pastors, Jerry Tom and Ron Harvey[53] (see Appendix B). I recorded the interview in person at the Window Rock Church of God office. I have included both the ceremony described by a traditional medicine man in the Navajo newspaper and the pastors' description of the way they performed the ceremony in a contextualized fashion in the 1980s.

Critical Contextualization
Reflecting upon Hiebert's model of critical contextualization, the phenomenological examination happens internally in this case, as in the others. The ceremony had been contextualized previously but, due to criticism from locals and church people, was discontinued. This is an example of how a practice that might have been disallowed by expatriate missionaries or more assimilated Natives can be effectively contextualized to result in an effective outreach which unifies the church. This case is unique in that, rather than a purely Native tradition being contextualized, it is a merging of two very traditional celebrations – the Navajo 'Squaw Dance' or Enemy Way Ceremony and the Pentecostal camp meeting.

I learned that there were several touch points that suggested to the people that the Enemy Way Ceremony could be contextualized with Pentecostal worship. These touch points include brush arbor, healing prayer, spiritual warfare, and benevolence as an outreach.

Brush Arbor

The first touch point would be the use of a brush arbor, which has an important role in outdoor Pentecostal evangelism and worship. This practice of using a brush arbor, though used for reason of lack of funds for a facility in the early days of the fledgling Pentecostal movement, put the people outside in plain view of the community to demonstrate their interesting worship.[54] This reality was also a

---

[53] Jerry Tom and Ron Harvey, 'Window Rock Church of God Interview', Window Rock (2008).

[54] See also the use of the brush arbor by Assembly of God Native Americans in Tarango's account. Tarango's responsible research traces the loss of community relationship when the alternative camp meeting replaces the powwow, (Tarango, '"Choosing the Jesus Way:" the Assemblies of God's Home Missions to American Indians and the Development of a Pentecostal Indian Identity', p. 127). See also Lingenfelter's treatment of community ritual as a cohesive social

powerful force in terms of evangelism as the Window Rock group reached their community. Now they enjoy a comfortable air-conditioned facility, and those who drive by do not know what is going on inside. The Window Rock Church of God does continue to be a visible witness in the community as a leader in public civic events and outreach.

Healing Prayer

Prayer for the healing of physical and emotional trauma has been an important part of Pentecostal worship since its inception. The integration of a healing ceremony with Pentecostal worship is a given, and Pentecostalism has always made use of sacred objects such as anointing oil, anointed cloths, and other touch points for healing. The use of candy in healing the sick is legendary, though rarely mentioned.

Spiritual Warfare

The act of aggressively going forward to deliver souls from the bondage and adverse effects of violent trauma (especially demonic activity) is an important part of Pentecostal practice which often involves public demonstrations such as Jericho Marches and the destruction of sacred objects of other spiritual influence (see Acts 19.18-20).

Benevolence as an Outreach

In keeping with Pentecostalism's natural connection to the poor and disenfranchised, the contextualized Enemy Way Ceremony of Window Rock included daily open feasting, which fed a community and met the needs of a large number of families.[55]

Ceremony and Scripture

Certainly the participants of the Enemy Way Ceremony can look to the Old and New Testaments to observe scriptural bases for feasts and celebrations. The Day of Pentecost stands as one example where the New Testament and the Spirit of God sanctioned and blessed such events. The Navajo, however, do not feel a need to find a biblical basis for a beneficial practice that was given to them

---

connector (Lingenfelter, *Agents of Transformation: A Guide for Effective Cross-Cultural Ministry*, p. 166).
   [55] Tom and Harvey, 'Window Rock Church of God Interview'.

by the Creator in times before they met Christ. They see the Enemy Way Ceremony as an opportunity to join the gospel with their families and friends and celebrate the power of deliverance through Jesus Christ.

Comparison

The contextualized Enemy Way Ceremony includes participant experiences that may be compared to those encountered in any number of spiritual retreats and rituals in the Protestant tradition such as Emmaus Walk or *Tres Dias*. This is an adaptation of an indigenous ceremony that takes Christian themes and contextualizes them in the Navajo way. The contextual Enemy Way Ceremony, however, is unique in serving the needs of a suffering war veteran. The most significant difference is the substitution of the pastor in place of the medicine man, but it is critically important to make the spiritual impartation consistent with the Christian and Pentecostal context and to guard against syncretism.

Transformed Practice

The fully transformed version of the Enemy Way Ceremony by the Navajo Pentecostals of Window Rock remains as a powerful testimony of contextualization in the collective memory of the believers of that region, and due to the continued connection to the contextual movement through visiting ministries, might be revived again. It is clear that denominational officials and local church members of other congregations, who were critical in that day, did not approve of such activity and felt it was syncretistic. Only time will tell whether the Church will remember the wonderful harvest and choose to revive it.

> But not only did we use the concept of squaw dance – it's not even called squaw dance, it's another name that means 'the Enemy Way' – it was the Anglo who came and looked at the women dancing with the men and called it squaw dance. And then they called it 'the enemy way' because just as pastor said, it reconnects mind, soul, and body of a person. And I guess it was a sacred thing, it was a holy thing until alcohol got into it, and drugs got into it, and sexual immorality got into it. And that's why, when the churches looked at it, they saw it as a demonic thing, so when we did it in the 80s you can imagine how controversial it was back then.

But people came first because of the food – breakfast, afternoon lunch, evening lunch, and after service food. It was all given out for free. At one point here in Window Rock we butchered over twenty-seven sheep just that week. They just loved all of the food. The tribal workers would come down here just to eat free, and while they were eating, we would get the attention of the people and say, 'Can I tell you about Jesus?' And we began to witness to this people. So while they are eating they are listening to different testimonies of what God has done in different lives. And so in the evening they would come back to join us in our services, and then to eat again after service. So it all centers around a fellowship of breaking bread; so when they come back, they bring their families and it all grew bigger and bigger. But at the same time, churches around us gave us problems because they were against it.[56]

These practices, though varied in their tribal origins and character, are similar examples of how Pentecostal Native churches are making decisions on how to include or not include certain traditional practices. I have generally included descriptions of how the Natives are carrying out Hiebert's model with spiritual variations. In the next chapter I will examine the theological ramifications of this behavior and what it might mean for the larger Native American Contextual Movement and its affiliates in Pentecostal denominations.

---

[56] Tom and Harvey, 'Window Rock Church of God Interview'.

4

THEOLOGICAL REFLECTIONS IN THE LIGHT OF CONTEXTUALIZATION THEORY

In the first issue of the *Journal of North American Institute for Indigenous Theological Studies* (NAIITS), 2003, a statement of faith is articulated that clearly outlines the American Indian Contextual Movements' (AICM) stand concerning syncretism.

> Theologically, we are strongly opposed to syncretism in any form, specifically when cultural practice in any way begins to encroach on the authority of God's Word and in particular, the work of the cross. Our aim is to provide a theological framework for defining syncretism.[1]

The mention of Scripture is important. This statement was published some time after Twiss' response to the Christian and Missionary Alliance (CMA) in his *Dancing Our Prayers*,[2] and no doubt reflects the convictions that Twiss came away with from that interchange. The AICM finds support from David Hesselgrave and Edward Rommen, citing the following statement: 'There is a need to use existing forms that can be baptized and pressed into the service of Christ if the gospel is not denied in the process'.[3] This is not just a permissive possibility of contextualization, but a statement for a need of such. Also, there is a direct endorsement of agreement with a particular missiological perspective, as they quote

---

[1] Jacobs, Twiss, and Leblanc, 'Culture, Christian Faith and Error', p. 6.
[2] Twiss, *Dancing Our Prayers*.
[3] Jacobs, Twiss, and Leblanc, 'Culture, Christian Faith and Error', p. 6.

Charles Kraft, who notes the importance of theological thinking
that takes place in the human environment but originates with God.

> We implicitly and explicitly committed ourselves to the Prot-
> estant Bible as the revelation of God and, therefore normative in
> regard to the understandings we advocate concerning God and
> His relationships with and desires for humans. He it is who orig-
> inated, oversees and keeps working all that exists. *We see, then,*
> *God as existing above and outside of culture yet working through culture in*
> *His interactions with human beings* (emphasis added).[4]

The Native American Contextual Movement Addresses Syncretism

Kraft's perspective represents the belief that God works through
culture, which is important for the contextual movement. Exactly
why my Native American colleagues adapted Kraft rather than
Hiebert is not particularly clear, but may not be significant since
Kraft endorses Hiebert's model of critical contextualization.[5] However, the preference for Kraft may have something to do with what
some call his 'high view of culture'.

The CMA representatives who opposed Twiss, prompting his
response in *Dancing Our Prayers*, expressed a critique of Kraft publicly by saying, 'Kraft's position is unacceptable to those who accept
the authority of Scripture'.[6] They are referring to Kraft's statement:

> God takes into account the relativity of the human situation and
> that human accountability is relevant to the extent of revelation-
> al materials received. God adjusts his expectations to the cultural
> patterns of each society.[7]

If Kraft means by this that God deals directly and relationally
with cultures, then his view corresponds to Native beliefs, and
hence, explains part of the reason why they want to cite Kraft in
their statements. Twiss' definition of syncretism is descriptive:

---

[4] Charles H. Kraft, *Anthropology for Christian Witness* (Maryknoll: Orbis Books,
1996), p. 6; Jacobs, Twiss, and Leblanc, 'Culture, Christian Faith and Error'.

[5] Kraft, *Anthropology for Christian Witness*, p. 377.

[6] C&MA, *Boundary Lines: The Issue of Christ, Indigenous Worship and Native
American Culture*, p. 12.

[7] C.H. Kraft, *Christianity in Culture* (Maryknoll: Orbis Books, 1984), p. 125.

Syncretism can be described as a way of thinking that says by performing or participating in a particular religious ceremony or practice, you can alter the essential human spiritual condition in the same way that Jesus does, through His death on a cross, burial, and resurrection from the dead, because they are parallel truths and both equally acceptable in the eyes of God; thus can be considered the same thing and combined together. Theologically, syncretism states or implies a Native ceremony can cleanse the soul from sin in the same way the work of Jesus Christ does; or that performing Native ceremonies can heal sickness, perform miracles and bridge the sin barrier separating sinful human beings from a holy God because they are parallel truths from the same source. It is assigning the same weight of power and authority to unbiblical Native religious beliefs and ceremony that you do to the revelation of truth found in the Word of God.[8]

In a similar way, R. Daniel Shaw defines syncretism as

an incompatible mixture of Christianity and local beliefs and traditions. The question is, incompatible with what? The answer is God's Word. So if the Bible is the criteria against which we evaluate these practices, then syncretism becomes a moot point, especially in light of the extreme contextualization in much of American Christianity and the phenomenal amount of syncretism that results.[9]

In this statement, Shaw joins Twiss in affirming the primacy of the Word of God and then points out that syncretism is not a problem that pertains only to Native Americans.

Fear and Prejudice

Pentecostals, both early and contemporary, have experienced certain mistreatment due to the use of sacred objects. This is partially due to the unique position of Pentecostal theology. Though Pentecostals are thoroughly Bible centered, and many Pentecostal denominations are members of the National Association of Evangelicals (Pentecostals have even served as presidents of NAE), Pente-

---

[8] Twiss, *Dancing Our Prayers*, pp. 23-24.
[9] R. Daniel Shaw, 'Contextualization' Personal Email communication (2009).

costal theology is still more Eastern than Western, having roots in the Pietistic Tradition, and probably having more in common with Roman Catholicism than Fundamentalism.[10] This puts the Pentecostal movement in a unique position to join Native Americans and potentially have more unity with them even than Catholicism once enjoyed.

Most of the fear of syncretism and prejudice revolves around sacred objects. The question is still asked, 'Can God redeem objects that were once used in pagan practice?' The following admonition is published in NAIITS journal:

> Some Native American believers also object to believers using objects, styles or patterns of worship that may have been used by non-Christians in their own pagan worship ceremonies. While they are indeed certainly correct in rejecting the use of drugs to facilitate communion with God since this is condemned in the Scriptures, it would be most inappropriate to forbid all other practices as well. The pagan use of musical instruments, incense, meditation, water and a myriad of other objects and practices does not mean that all such items can never be used to worship God. Rather they ought to be *reclaimed, sanctified and transformed* for God's glory.[11]

Reducing fear and prejudice regarding the use of sacred objects and the use of traditional practices in a Christian worship setting is necessary if denominational Native American ministries intend to go forward at this time. The above discussion is ongoing throughout the Church and will not be resolved by prohibitions. Non-Natives must try to understand the issues and also the importance of trust in the discerning of practices in worship by Native leaders. The ideas of reclamation, sanctification, and transformation will be used as descriptive levels in how contextualization is practiced by Native Americans.

---

[10] Steven Land, *Pentecostal Spirituality* (JPTSup, 1; Sheffield: Sheffield Academic Press, 1993), p. 30.

[11] Douglas Hayward, 'Foundations for Critical Contextualization: Preliminary Considerations for Doing Contextualization among First Nations Christians', *Journal of North American Institute for Indigenous Theological Studies* 1.1 (2003), p. 48.

Levels in Native American Pentecostal Contextualization

I will now reflect theologically, anthropologically, and missiologically on what appears to be taking place in the Native Pentecostal churches I have observed. I will interact with the literature and data in a descriptive way.

Reclaiming Traditional Experiences, Sanctifying Functional Practices, and Transforming Spiritual Experiences for God's Glory

The words used in the official theological statement of the Native American contextual movement – 'reclaimed, sanctified and transformed' – describe in a general way the processes that my data suggests. They coincide with what the contextual movement is trying to do to respond to the problem of syncretism.

Reclaiming Indian Traditions

One of the ways that the contextual movement intends to reclaim Indian traditions is through the use of objects and practices (excluding drugs). The contextual movement, in general, and my interviewees in particular, are concerned about the danger of neo-paganism. What they seek to do is not to exercise the type of 'wholesale rejection' that many missionaries have done.[12] Barnetson suggested in the interview that an initial benefit of smudging in the church context was 'embracing the practice';[13] this, it seems to me, would have a welcoming effect for traditional attendees that may not be believers. Brown refers to the 'traditional drum', which holds significance for Indians.[14] The circle is a universal symbol for Native Americans and is present at the first sight of a talking circle.[15] Dance is a universal symbol of prayer and ceremonies are filled with symbolism.[16]

These symbols hold as much significance for the critical observer as they do for the insider, only in a more negative sense. The missionaries, both past and present who see these symbols, are reminded of the negative spiritual connotations from pagan labeling,

---

[12] Hiebert, Shaw, and Tienou, *Understanding Folk Religion*, p. 20.
[13] Barnetson, 'Telephone Interview with Randy Barnetson'.
[14] Brown, 'Telephone Interview with Larry "Grizz" Brown'.
[15] Lundy, 'Interview'.
[16] Bear-Barnetson, 'Cheryl Bear Barnetson Interview'.

and coupled with fear and prejudice, prompt wholesale rejection. This is one of the weaknesses of an external model such as that of Paul Hiebert. On the inside, the presence of traditional Native practices in the Church can also have a negative effect for those trained under the non-Native missionaries that may have attached certain fear to the practices. Insiders who are traditional unbelievers may experience a positive effect in the embrace of the practice, even to the extent that it may recall precious tribal memories and values, even connecting with a loved one or respected elder. At the very least, there is an overarching awareness that the Christians respect the tribal people and not only love their souls, but their lives as well.

The phenomenological analysis in this way is done by the traditional people themselves, rather than by an outside critique. Previously, analysis has been done by the Native leaders. This was achieved through their process of critical contextualization and decision-making in order to allow the practice to be done in the Church.

Sanctifying Functional Practices

The 'excluded middle' to which Hiebert refers is the area that folk religions satisfy, and that Westerners, though usually unrecognized, have in their own folk religions.[17] In Barnetson's description of smudging, he points out that smudging is generally understood by the Indian population as having a cleansing function.[18] Whether this cleansing is perceived to be actual or not will be overshadowed by the emphasis people place on the higher cleansing that Christ has provided through his redemptive work on the cross, which is only symbolized through the smoke.

The theological idea of sanctification can be defined through the use of the New Testament word *hagiazo*, which means 'to consecrate' or 'to sanctify', generally meaning to dedicate someone or something to God's service.[19] Just as feeding the hungry through relief efforts satisfies a specific function and physical need, while

---

[17] P.G. Hiebert, 'The Flaw of the Excluded Middle', *Missiology: An International Review* 10.1 (1982)

[18] Barnetson, 'Telephone Interview with Randy Barnetson'.

[19] O. Procksch, 'hagiázō', in G. Kittel and G. Friedrich, *The Theological Dictionary of the New Testament Abridged in One Volume* (Grand Rapids, MI: Eerdmans, 1985), p. 17.

answering a higher significance in obeying the law of love, in a similar way certain traditional practices fulfill the personal needs of Native Americans. The Native American Contextual Movement, as represented by my Pentecostal colleagues, believes that some of these functional practices can be utilized.

Transforming Spiritual Experiences for God's Glory

What is happening in these Native American contexts is not just inclusion of tribal culture. There are changes taking place in the minds and hearts of the worshipers. At the very least worshipers catch a visual idea that the God of the Christian Church loves their culture. Traditional people are taught that ceremonies are given to their people by God. The God of their mothers and fathers can now become their God through a form of Christianity that honors their age-old traditions and does not suggest that European practices are necessary for acceptance by God.

Beyond the visual reality that God loves their culture, there is an awareness, based on the significance of traditional cultural ceremonies, that this God not only loves their people but also truly wants to fulfill their needs. On a deeper level, through a new expanded meaning of their traditions taught by their church leaders, the worshipers receive revelation of the one true God in a way that they understand and can appreciate. Their sincere practice in worship, coupled with their faith in Jesus Christ, brings the grace of God to work in their lives, and the blessings of grace are communicated through them to other Native Americans.

Dawn Brown, wife of Larry 'Grizz' Brown, although aware of the cultural significance of the hand drum and the symbolic use of the drum in Pentecostal Christian praise and worship, was unaware of the deep spiritual experience which she would undergo that would ultimately answer her questions of purpose and vocation.[20] This illustrates the multi-leveled benefits of Native American contextualization, particularly in the Pentecostal context. Larry Brown describes:

> There are more hand drums in our Native community than there are big drums because, like I said, a hand drum is very personalized. Linda Prince travels with a group called a hundred

---

[20] Brown, 'Telephone Interview with Larry "Grizz" Brown'.

and twenty drums, and they literally carry a hundred and twenty drums with them. I have been involved in contextualized ministries for a few years, and my wife has not had the privilege of coming with me on any of my trips. Back around 2001, I think it was, my wife came with me to this reservation, and Lynda Prince was there; they passed out a hundred and twenty hand drums, and one was given to my wife. And then she added her worship and the beat on the drum given to her; there was a transformation that came over her. And I believe that when she was drumming, the Lord gave her a very clear vision on not only what he had called me to but also what he had called us to. And it was when she was playing the drum that it got into her spirit the understanding that was going on.

I've heard that from a lot of people; even the day before yesterday I heard it said, 'I never felt the presence of the Holy Spirit like I did when I was drumming and dancing'. And I think one of the reasons is, where the Spirit of the Lord is, there's liberty. And liberty is cause for rejoicing, and a lot of people have been taught in a lot of cases to worship within a certain realm of allowances and they feel restricted, and they don't feel free, and it's unfortunate. I have experienced it, and I never stayed in those circles for too long because I have the Holy Spirit, and I am free and I want to walk in freedom, I'm going to run in freedom, I am going to dance in freedom and I will invite people to join me in that circle of freedom. And my wife experienced that freedom come upon her the first time that she drummed; and now she and another group of wives from my group will stand with us, they will stand behind us as we are seated in the drum, and they will rattle along with us, and sing a long with us. So they are a very vital part of our group.[21]

There is also clearly transformation taking place in Taylor's experience with his use of language. According to the Cherokee Language and Culture Preservation Bill, language is 'the single most important attribute of cultural persistence'.[22] Important models of

---

[21] Brown, 'Telephone Interview with Larry "Grizz" Brown'. Part of Brown's statement is cited above, but it bears repeating here.

[22] Green and Fernandez, *The British Museum Encyclopedia of Native North America*, p. 91.

language contextualization are taking place in Native American Pentecostal churches and gatherings. Stephan Bevans' models of contextualization can be used as a way to describe what Taylor is doing, as well as what is going on more generally in this Native American movement.[23] Taylor's concern for tribal protocol seems to follow in the 'anthropological model', where cultural identity is preserved in a Christian context. The inter-tribal use of language could be viewed as being more in line with what Bevans refers to as the 'translation model', where it is more a concern to be Christian first, then Indian. The translation model is more in line with what can be found in the more conservative and assimilated contexts.

The Contributions of a Pneumatological Pentecostal/Charismatic Theology of Religions

While Bevans' models of contextualization are helpful for examining the continuum within the contextual movement, Hiebert and Kraft go further in helping me describe both in the literature and the data the processes of contextualization that are going on. The formal statements of the movement and the arguments that can be found in their literature emphasize Scripture a bit more than what is to be found in the data.[24]

In the data, the interviewees tend to use a model more like the Wesleyan Quadrilateral, which is a combination of tradition, reason, Scripture, and experience.[25] By that I mean that the interviewees had Providential experiences that caused them to reflect on their Indian heritage, and at some point they were able to see in Scripture that what they were doing was good and reasonable in light of their Indian-ness, not necessarily because they were laying the grid of Scripture upon the whole of Native American culture.

It could be argued that they are truly following Hiebert and Shaw's critical contextualization model, or a particular 'critical hermeneutic', such as is found in Bosch, for surely they are carefully

---

[23] Stephen Bevans, *Models of Contextual Theology* (Maryknoll: Orbis Books, 1992), p. 47.

[24] Jacobs, Twiss, and Leblanc, 'Culture, Christian Faith and Error'; Twiss, *Dancing Our Prayers*.

[25] D.A.D. Thorsen, *Wesleyan Quadrilateral: Scripture, Tradition, Reason & Experience as a Model of Evangelical Theology* (Grand Rapids, MI: Zondervan Pub. House, 1990), p. 1.

studying Scripture, praying with the Church, and making critical calls as to what is appropriate and what is syncretistic.[26]

A helpful theory which intersects with what the Native Americans are doing in their practices is a Pentecostal Theology of Religions. This theory has developed in particular fashion, beginning with Walter Hollenweger's theory of Pentecostal theology in 1972. Followed by contributions by Harvey Cox, Clark Pinnock, Veli-Matti Kärkkäinen, and A. Yong,[27] the theory is built upon a pneumacentric approach which avoids the so called 'Christological impasse'[28] and acknowledges that God is working in other religions before Christianity comes. The pneumatological theology of religions asks the religion about its spiritual experiences, what utilitarian benefits are found in the religion and finally, what connections can be found in cosmology.[29] There are several important features of the Pentecostal Theology of Religions that resonate with the Indian contextual situation.

God is in the Traditional Religion

Representatives of the contextual movement argue that God revealed himself to the Native Americans through a variety of aspects of their traditional religion. This idea appears throughout my interviews and data, and I must honor my interviewees' belief that this is not just animistic or pantheistic folk religion based on superstition. They go so far as to do word studies and exegesis to demonstrate that God was revealing himself to their people and through their ceremonies before the Great Book and Christ came.[30]

---

[26] Hiebert, *Anthropological Insights for Missionaries*, pp. 186-92; Bosch, *Transforming Mission: Paradigm Shifts in Theology of Mission*, pp. 23-24; Hiebert, Shaw, and Tienou, *Understanding Folk Religion*; Shaw and Van Engen, *Communicating God's Word in a Complex World: God's Truth or Hocus Pocus?*

[27] Cox, *Fire from Heaven: The Rise of Pentecostal Spirituality and the Reshaping of Religion in the Twenty-First Century*; Pinnock, *Flame of Love: A Theology of the Holy Spirit*; Kärkkäinen, *An Introduction to the Theology of Religions*; Yong, *Discerning the Spirit(s)*.

[28] I would define a Christological impasse as the overemphasis of the second person of the Trinity to the exclusion of the Third, which prevents potential common understanding through dialogue concerning Holy Spirit/Great Spirit.

[29] Yong, *Discerning the Spirit(s)*, p. 222.

[30] Taylor, 'Personal Interview'; Barnetson, 'Telephone Interview with Randy Barnetson'; Ron Harvey, 'Window Rock Church of God Interview', Window Rock (2008).

Spirit Emphasis

A Pentecostal theology of religions 'begins by focusing on phenomenological commonalities (Divine presence)', then the 'task of discernment therefore necessarily moves us both logically and existentially from categories of Divine presence to categories of Divine activity'.[31] This prevents the Christological impasse with which traditionalists may have a problem in initial evangelistic discussions.

Cosmology

Cosmology may be the most powerful category for engaging Native American worldview with Christianity. I have already mentioned the spatial interests and importance in Native thought. This feature holds much potential for this topic, due to the need and constant call for a spatial approach to Native American culture over and against a temporal, external perspective. A spatial approach not only avoids the stereotypical ideas of Western histories, but also speaks in ways that are more consistent with the Native worldview that is vitally connected to spatial concerns. The relationship of the people to the land and the future of the cosmos need to be explored in all interreligious discussions between Natives and non-Natives. Space would not permit me to develop the diversity of understanding of cultures across the geographical landscape. This is the third level of Yong's dimensions, which enables Pentecostals to have discussion with Native Americans about the present and future without being trapped in temporalities.[32]

Spiritual Discernment

Dan Lundy speaks of discerning the spirits in regard to the degree of contextualization in which his congregation should be involved. He states, 'Once when a so-called "seer" came and wanted to read people and told them that regalia and smudging was required according to Scripture, they were [*sic*, he was] removed'.[33] The Pentecostal practice of discernment is active in these cases and can be misunderstood by the untrained observer as nothing more than subjectivity. 'Discerning the spirits' is an extremely important practice in contextualizing ceremonies that have been connected with

---

[31] Yong, *Discerning the Spirit(s)*, pp. 226-27.
[32] Yong, *Discerning the Spirit(s)*, p. 31.
[33] Lundy, 'Interview'.

shamanic practice and is included in a Pentecostal theology of religions.

A Trinitarian approach, which has gained much support recently,[34] is very effective among Native Americans, who celebrate a plurality in God. Next to their strong patriotic commitments, their Trinitarian commitment also was amazing in terms of its strength across the corpus of my data.

Anthropological Reflections: A Revision of Hiebert's Model of Critical Contextualization

The overall strength of Hiebert's model lies in its essential outline of approach to a needful subject in missiology. In this section I will reflect on the strengths and weaknesses for Native American Pentecostal application and how Hiebert's model could be revised to fit this context.

Phenomenological Examination

My outsider's examination of the 'phenomena' reveals the external nature of Hiebert's model, and naturally so. There is no way a Euro-American missionary can comprehend the full significance or the diversity of Native practices. This step must be replaced with the insiders' welcome to a world they know. Then they will be brought from 'the known to the unknown' in the worship experience. Examination must also be replaced with participation. Only then can the objective process be moved from an etic to an emic, or a more nativistic approach.

Testing Beliefs and Practices

According to my observations, the way in which the Native American Pentecostals examine their practices in light of biblical truth is undergirded by the awareness that God is in the traditional religion and that they are involved in a progressive revelation. Perhaps more importantly, they do not possess the suspicion and prejudice with which white Protestants struggle. This presupposition that the God of the Bible has given the initial ceremonies and rituals makes the tests of reality easier due to the fact that it is *their* particular reality. The American Indian theological tradition as found in such volumes as Brown's and Neihardt's works (and others) integrate the

---

[34] Kärkkäinen, *An Introduction to the Theology of Religions*, p. 353.

cross into a theology of sacrifice and serve as previous examples of how Christianity can be viewed in this context.[35] The interesting Pentecostal variation on this tradition that was largely and conveniently Roman Catholic proceeds with a spiritual discernment by the pastoral leaders as well as community members, who prayerfully weigh out which practices are to be included and which are not.

Evaluating Old Beliefs

Native American leaders utilize biblical material from poetic, propositional, and narrative texts. In this it appears that they are employing the range of biblical genres in the task. For musical instruments they point to references from the Psalms of Praise; for smudging they refer to Old and New Testament references to incense, as well as Lukan references to Paul and purification rituals; and underlying it all is the Mars Hill speech in which the redemptive analogy is derived. These practices are subjected to the light of biblical truth. This seems to be developing into a Native American Lukan Pentecostal hermeneutic, though this is a tentative analysis.

Ministries That Transform Individuals and Congregations

In order to move from where they are to where God wants them to be, these Native Americans are especially interested in the effect of various practices and their effect on contextualized behavior. This has a strong impact on their traditional and unchurched family and friends. They enjoy attending powwows and are even honored to be invited by traditional people to perform their 'Jesus songs' by their drum teams who normally provide worship drum praise for their local church services in the powwow performance and contests.

In further evangelistic efforts, they delight in doing cultural demonstrations in international contexts abroad, where they dance and drum their 'Jesus songs' before large gatherings of indigenous peoples.[36] They see this as an opportunity that traditional Protestant missions do not enjoy, and also view it as a prophetic calling issued by God directly to them as once again being 'host peoples' in the last days.

---

[35] Neihardt, *When the Tree Flowered: The Story of Eagle Voice, a Sioux Indian*; Neihardt, *Black Elk Speaks*; Brown, *The Sacred Pipe: Black Elk's Account of the Seven Rites of the Oglala Sioux*.

[36] Twiss, *One Church Many Tribes*, pp. 191-213.

Locally, they enjoy worshiping in the 'Indian way' and continue to celebrate their newfound freedom to worship the Creator as they integrate their Indian-ness as well as Christianity in relevant ways. All of this appears to be a 'shorter way' than Hiebert's model that bypasses both the cultural misunderstandings and 'Christological impasse'. Due to the involvement of indigenous leaders in the process, issues of protocol are avoided, and European residue is more easily removed from the gospel presentations. Hiebert has provided a wonderful process that need only be adjusted to a more internal model enabling a strategic approach within the Native American community.

I have demonstrated in this chapter that there appears to be not only a three-stage process to the way Native Americans contextualize their worship practices, but there also seems to be a three-fold dimension to the official way they state what they are doing. I have also pointed out how a Pentecostal theology of religions holds promise for an understanding that is more congruent with the Native worldview and approach. In order to find continuity missiologically, I have demonstrated how Hiebert's model of critical contextualization might be modified in the light of both Native and Pentecostal contributions.

So what does all this mean for the growth of Native American Pentecostals and their churches? What benefit does contextualization have for the future of Native American Pentecostalism? In Chapter 5, I will explore the relevance of contextualized practices for the churches.

5

RELEVANCE OF NATIVE AMERICAN PRACTICES FOR CONTEXTUALIZED BEHAVIOR IN PENTECOSTAL CHURCHES

The context of my data is quite different than what is normally envisioned in missiological treatments of contextualization. This is largely due to the internal nature of the phenomenological analysis and the high degree of trained leadership among this group that, despite the long exposure to the gospel and their internal application of biblical principles to their worship styles, is still largely treated as a mission field. This causes me to reflect on several realities observed in my interviews and observations.

Native Americans are not a recently reached people group with minimally trained leaders. Most of my interviewees are Bible college graduates, and in some cases seminary trained pastors. Most of my interviewees at some time after their conversion focused away from their Indian-ness and served as pastors of non-Native congregations for a time. In a few cases, they participated in a Native American service where practices were contextualized and were called by the Holy Spirit to re-embrace their Native identities and move to a more holistic expression of their true selves in ministry for Christ. These testimonies were both deeply touching and troubling. They were touching in that the grace of God was faithful to lead them to a truer experience of both their identity in Christ and a more honest approach to ministry. They were troubling in the sense that they have been warned and even persecuted for the steps they have taken to reach the traditional people, many of whom are their rela-tives.[1]

This initial reality casts a new light on approaches such as Hiebert's 'contextualization steps'. The objective act of missionaries evaluating culture phenomenologically is not what is going on in the Native American contextual movement. Rather, trained Native pastors are biblically examining their own cultures and putting key rituals and ceremonies into practice. The question 'How are Chris-tians to respond?'[2] is answered by, 'These are the Christians'. They are examining their practices phenomenologically.[3] The mistake of treating Native Americans as a perpetual mission field is a major barrier to unity in the body of Christ.[4] Native Americans are mak-ing conclusions about which practices to use working from an emic rather than an etic perspective.[5]

While they are not short on Scriptural basis for what they do, they prefer to point to the pre-Christian evidences of God in their midst, giving and working through traditional ceremonies to lead their people eventually to Christ in much the same way that the Hebrew feasts pointed Israel to God. This idea of Native peoples being tribes that God visited before the coming of the 'Great Book' is very prevalent in the American Indian Contextual discussion.[6] This is why Richardson's 'redemptive analogy' seems so helpful to them.[7] In this sense, it is not a search for ways to 'Christianize' cer-tain 'pagan practices', but fresh ways to learn from and about God.[8] Their view of God already being in the traditions complicates Hiebert's approach, and calls for a modification. They are experi-encing a fundamentally different type of missiological transfor-mation, as they apply incarnational principles to the contextualiza-tion process. They are essentially applying their knowledge of God, acquired in multiple ways, to the theological process within their context.

---

[1] Taylor, 'Personal Interview'; Lundy, 'Interview'.

[2] Hiebert, *Anthropological Insights for Missionaries*, p. 176.

[3] Taylor, 'Personal Interview'.

[4] Twiss, *One Church Many Tribes*, p. 58.

[5] Hiebert, *Cultural Anthropology*, p. 413.

[6] Gavriel Gefen, 'Re-Contextualization: Restoring the Biblical Message to a Jewish Israeli Context', *Journal of North American Institute for Indigenous Theological Studies* 4 (2006), pp. 5-28.

[7] Richardson, *Eternity in Their Hearts*.

[8] Taylor, 'Personal Interview'.

It is important to note that this represents doing theology from above, as Van Engen puts it. Rather than a teacher or missionary guiding them through the process, their own leaders do it with discerning understanding guided by Scripture.[9] This is what Shaw and Van Engen are doing as they seek to provide theological and cultural insight into appropriating Scripture to local contexts where God has always been known and God's Word needs to be appropriated.[10] My interviewees are not predisposed to reject their 'old ways', neither do they accept them uncritically, nor were they strictly following Hiebert's approach. Barnetson is giving basis for smudging through a practice in Pentecostalism. He sees the smudging as a transformed practice much like anointing with oil. Though anointing with oil can be found in the Old Testament (despite there often being more smoke than oil), the Gospels (Mk 6.13), and the Epistles (Jas 5.14), it is Barnetson's interest more to point out the connection between traditional smudging and 'this land', contrasting it to olive oil's origin in Europe.[11] This reveals that a critical contextualization for Native Americans must possess a spatial approach or one that makes a connection with the land. A similar case has been made by Shaw, who refers to a transformed healing practice of the Samo, describing the process as a 'cognitive environment interfaced with biblical truth to create a whole new approach to prayer for the sick'.[12]

What Practices Are Being Contextualized?

The first part of my study has to do with ascertaining which practices Native Pentecostal churches are using. To answer the first part of my quest was to enquire as to the historical examples of Natives

---

[9] Hiebert, Shaw, and Tienou, *Understanding Folk Religion*, p. 29.

[10] Shaw and Van Engen, *Communicating God's Word in a Complex World: God's Truth or Hocus Pocus?*, p. 195.

[11] Barnetson, 'Telephone Interview with Randy Barnetson'.

[12] R. Daniel Shaw, 'A Samo Theology of Mediumship: A Case Study of Local Theologizing and Global Reflection', in Carole M. Cusack and Christopher H. Hartney (eds.), *The International Festschrift for Garry W. Trompf* (Leiden: Brill, 2009), p. 15. '"Cognitive studies" is the result of investigations largely coming out of anthropology, linguistics, and psychology. It is the result of researchers attempting to understand how the brain processes information' (R. Daniel Shaw, 'Of Grass, Food, and Hospitality: The Role of Cognitive Studies in the Translation/Communication Task', *Scriptura* 96 [2007]), pp. 501-522 (501).

contextualizing traditional practice in order to utilize it in worship. The examples are few. Early in the study, I became aware that Stomp Dances were still being practiced on Baptist Church properties in Oklahoma. The term 'still' led me to search the history of Cherokee missionaries, and I learned that Stomp Dances had been used as early as the Trail of Tears period.

The other historical example was one of more recent history. The Navajo Pentecostals of Window Rock had contextualized the Enemy Way in the 1980s (see Appendix B). There were no other practices that came to my attention, although I feel certain they had been contextualized in the privacy of tribal life.

By doing this research, I hope to enable the Native American Pentecostal community to proceed with an integrated Christian witness for worldwide evangelism. Discovering Native American Pentecostal churches and interviewing their leaders resulted in a clear group of practices. These practices did not include the use of tobacco. This was not surprising due to the far-reaching influence of the Holiness movement that gave rise to Pentecostalism, and the existence of tobacco prohibitions in Pentecostal statements of faith. I was surprised to find that the sweat lodge was not included as a contexualized practice. While a few Pentecostals speak of praying in the sweat lodge, it was not mentioned by any of my interviewees.

I have identified six common practices/ceremonies that are currently being contextualized in Native Pentecostal churches. The practices that can be found in these churches, including those I presented as case studies in Chapter 4, are: use of language, smudging, drums and rattles, dance, talking circles, and the Enemy Way. Another aspect of the question, 'What practices can actually be used in order to provide meaningful worship while at the same time avoiding syncretism?', speaks to the particular practices that are conducive to Pentecostal worship. Dance has been found in Pentecostal worship since its inception, and drums have been an important instrument in many Pentecostal churches, the exception being the most conservative holiness-Pentecostal churches that feel that drums are as syncretistic in relation to Native American churches as they were in Africa. The Eastern roots of Pentecostalism, with its incense and the use of sacred objects such as cloths and anointing oil, may account for smudging's acceptance in Pentecostal worship in North American contexts.[13] I have already discussed how talking circles are like small groups and support groups. Language and ceremony are the least conducive to Pentecostal worship, but language can be framed in Pentecostal ways. Pentecostals are very comfortable with festive celebrations and camp meetings that are conducive to ceremonies such as the Enemy Way.

In light of these identified practices, Native Pentecostal leaders may continue a discerning analysis, and a thoughtful reflection can provide answers to why these particular practices/ceremonies are the ones being utilized. Non-Natives and those who are interested in Native American ministry, can study these practices and observe further to become more oriented to Native practice and cultural understanding. The identification of a set number of ceremonies that are approved by Pentecostal worship leaders simplifies the bewilderment for those who observe Native practice and reduces fear and prejudice, making denominational working relationships smoother.

Hearing Pentecostal Native theologians describe the Christian elements found in Native traditional practices aids in the understanding of Native worldview by non-Natives. Such cultural awareness results in unity in the body of Christ and closer fellowship among Native American Christians who collectively celebrate their Indian-ness every time they worship.

How Are the Practices Being Contextualized?

There is no doubt that the existence of many more trained pastors in Native American churches and the high level of their training in comparison to the Removal period changes the ways that Natives contextualize. Yet, there is still a tremendous need for empowerment of Native pastors and educational opportunities to be multiplied for them. At present, Native pastors and members have access to resources, especially the internet, to study and reflect on the theological implications of their contextualization.

---

[13] Alexander, *Pentecostal Healing: Models in Theology and Practice*, pp. 82-83.

Redemptive Analogy

Most of my interviewees mentioned Don Richardson's redemptive analogy approach;[14] one referred to it as 'common ground ministry'. What is significant about Richardson, more than any other contextualization model, is the simple belief, based on the book of Acts, that God works with unreached and un-evangelized people groups through their religious quests. Taylor explains,

> Well, in my ministry I focus on all of them, but I think we probably excel in the dance, and the song. If you look at culture of Natives, especially my tribe, I teach three areas: there is a grey area of cultural practices, that you can look into, there are areas that are, you know demonic, and you want to stay away from them. And then there's a majority of areas in our culture that are, 'redeemable', and so I pray about them and I find the ones that have a great deal of spiritual content, historically, and see how they were practiced. Then, I contextualize them using the redemptive analogy approach to show those Natives that I'm trying to reach, just how much they are connected with God and so there's a number of dances.[15]

Bear-Barnetson extends the paradigm of Paul the Apostle from the brief Mars Hill narrative (Acts 17.16-32) to make the assertion that Paul did not blaspheme pagan deities and participated in purification ceremonies not required in Christian observance.[16] Kyle Taylor (Pawnee/Choctaw) believes that redemptive analogy has to do with contextualizing what is present in your particular tribal culture, not just any tribal culture.

> So those are the kinds of things that we major on in my ministry, which is named after my great-great grandpa, and we have to utilize those things that are already in the culture. We don't have to come up and compose any new songs, we don't have to come up and compose any new dances, we don't have to come up and compose any new stuff. God already put those things in the cul-

---

[14] Richardson, *Eternity in Their Hearts*.

[15] Taylor, 'Personal Interview'.

[16] Bear-Barnetson, 'Introduction to First Nations Ministry'.

ture, and we utilize those and that's the power of redemptive analogy.[17]

This is an interesting and thoroughly considered paradigm, serving as a theological model that is being used by Native Americans today. I have been successful in demonstrating that this is one way that Natives contextualize by both hearing them use this paradigm to explain what they do publicly and hearing them explain it in interview settings. It will be interesting to watch how this paradigm becomes either extended or discarded altogether as Native Pentecostals continue their theological reflection in light of these principles. Richardson is a veteran white missionary of the late colonial period; so Native American theologians may revise their preferred paradigm as they integrate a more post-colonial, indigenous theology.

Critical Contextualization

Analyzing the contextualization methods of Native American Pentecostals, I have attempted to frame the process in a way similar to Hiebert's critical contextualization model.[18] The model includes:

1. Phenomenological Analysis: This was done through examining the history of the practice and the examination of the data itself, which may have included a participant observation and/or interview material.

2. Ontological Reflections: This was carried out through the analysis of whatever Biblical material was used to support the ceremony or practice.

3. Critical Evaluation: The contextualized practice was described in detail and compared to the traditional version.

4. Missiological Transformations: Here I set forth the transformed practice in detail.

As a result, I have followed and honored this missiological theory, even if certain practices may not seem to conform completely to Hiebert's specific criteria. By this, I mean that the people do not feel that they have to proof-text Scripture in each examination. If a practice seems to be 'good' under the prayerful and biblically informed Native leaders' eyes, it may be allowed. Native American Pentecostals that I have observed feel these transformations are

---

[17] Taylor, 'Personal Interview'.
[18] Hiebert, Shaw, and Tienou, *Understanding Folk Religion*, p. 21.

warranted, and several are aware of Hiebert's theory. I observe this in the literature of the contextual movement's leaders and theologians who cite Hiebert, Kraft, and other missiologists. They use this awareness to inform what is primarily a Native approach to spirituality.

Native American Pentecostal Contextualization

I have attempted in this presentation to describe what Natives are *doing* rather than using Scripture as the primary source of their approach to making Native practices relevant in worship. It is not surprising that they do not use Scripture in the sometimes mechanical ways that Anglo evangelicals might, nor should it be a concern for non-Native outsiders like myself. Hiebert, Shaw, and Tiénou's comments are a bit narrow in the light of the Wesleyan Quadrilateral (reason, experience, tradition, and Scripture all contribute to what is considered 'knowing').[19] Theories of Pentecostal experience and affections, provide a 'view of spirituality which is the integration of beliefs, affections, and actions (of knowing, being and doing)'.[20] The Wesleyan and Pentecostal spiritualities acknowledge 'ways of knowing' that transcend, though do not deny, cognitive knowledge and formation. In the light of this, we can examine the data without a certain rigidity that might otherwise be forced upon a more typically evangelical context. The remarks regarding power would have to be redefined in the Pentecostal theology of Luke and Acts, and not misconstrued to be manipulation or the force of a traditional shaman.

A Native American Pentecostal Lukan Hermeneutic

Early in my interviewing of pastors, Richardson's 'redemptive analogy', based on Paul's speech at Mars Hill from Acts 17, emerged. I did not anticipate what I would later find as it unfolded in the discussions. Richardson's analogy and its source in Acts was not just a random passage, but was part of a larger descriptive biblical theology that is emerging in the Native American Contextual Movement through its leaders. What follows is a tentative analysis of what appears to be taking place in this development.

The following Scripture passages and Bear-Barnetson's treatment of them is an example, and since they are taken from an aca-

---

[19] Hiebert, Shaw, and Tienou, *Understanding Folk Religion*, pp. 379-80.
[20] Land, *Pentecostal Spirituality*, p. 41.

demic doctoral thesis, may serve as a foundation of what will be a future formal statement of the movement's explanation of their contextualized worship practices. It is significant that they are taken primarily from the book of Acts, in keeping with the ongoing conversation based on Richardson's redemptive analogy.

Acts 14-15

> In Acts, Hebrew Christianity is contextualized to fit Greek Gentiles (Acts 14). The issue of circumcision is a huge problem (at the Jerusalem Council) and Paul confronts the 'Judaizers' (Acts 15). Paul accuses them of adding to the Gospel, of promoting their Hebrew culture over gospel freedom. He tells the council that Greeks do not need to become Jewish in order to be Christians – they can remain uncircumcised. Paul tells us that culture should not be an obstacle for one to come to Christ. Paul is yet again a shining example of contextualization when he explains God to the Greeks using their own unknown God (Acts 17:22-34).[21]

It is clear, at this point, that Bear-Barnetson is using the Apostle Paul as a missionary model in her treatment of contextualization. She speaks of the missionary challenge and barrier as more than just a cultural one. It is that Judaizers are 'promoting their Hebrew culture over gospel freedom'. This is a significant connection in which she sees First Nations/Native Americans as being under the difficulty of Euro-American cultural promotion. In doing so, she is setting a trajectory that now, interestingly, connects Natives with Greeks, rather than Hebrews.

Acts 16

Bear-Barnetson then discusses Paul becoming all things to all people: 'contextualizing himself' is the term she uses to describe this action.

> In Acts 16, Paul circumcises a Gentile (Timothy) ... If this passage is not read missiologically, it does not make much sense. In Acts 11 Peter explains his visit with Cornelius, a Gentile, to the Jewish believers. The Jewish believers rightly corrected Peter based on their religious views stating that Peter entered a house

---

[21] Bear-Barnetson, 'Introduction to First Nations Ministry', p. 76.

of uncircumcised men and shared a meal: these actions were inappropriate for a Jew. (However, because of the Holy Spirit, Peter was able to persuade the Judaizers that God was responsible for his visit and he was not being disobedient). Based on their religious beliefs, the Jews were right to question Peter's actions. Therefore, if Paul wanted to minister to Jewish people, they would have every right to question why he was associating with Timothy, an uncircumcised man, and the ministry would not happen. Here we see Paul contextualizing Timothy at a painful cost in order to facilitate ministry. This precedent applies to First Nations ministry. Anyone who desires to perform ministry among First Nations people must contextualize himself or herself. It is not as palpable as circumcision, but perhaps it can be just as painful.[22]

Here, with the apostle Paul as a model, the Supervisor of the Native Foursquare Churches of Canada presents an exegesis to establish the basis of contextual ministry illustrated by Paul and Timothy. In it, the Apostle is submitting (Bear-Barnetson would say) to a purification ceremony that is not required in his Christianity of grace.

Acts 17.22-34

Bear-Barnetson further describes how Paul uses objects and words from another culture to preach Good News.

Acts 17 finds Paul in Athens waiting for Silas and Timothy. While walking around the city Paul '... was greatly distressed to see that the city was full of idols'. (17:16) In Acts 17:22, Paul stands up and speaks. The first thing he does is acknowlege that the Athenians are very religious. He does not begin by shaming them or being condescending but rather Paul opens a door of discussion. He begins with a compliment on their spirituality. The next topic Paul chooses is directly from the Athenian culture, '... An Unknown God ...'. (17:23) He employed something from their culture to bring about the Truth. Paul rejects the 'Unknown God' and reveals the True God, who is not contained in stone or wood. In fact, Paul takes on their idols without demeaning their gods but rather by explaining God's true

[22] Bear-Barnetson, 'Introduction to First Nations Ministry', pp. 131-32.

nature. He begins by giving God a description: Creator. How, in the form of a temple, can humans capture in a temple the One who made everything? How can humans equip the Creator who consistently supplies them life and breath, and everything? Then Paul does something truly beautiful. In Acts 17:28 he quotes their sacred writings, ... in his Hymn to Zeus. Paul quotes Greek poets elsewhere as well (see 1 Cor. 15:33; Titus 1:12 and notes). (NIV Study Bible) How often does one hear modern missionaries quoting ancient sources of the people to whom they are ministering? There is spirituality in every nation of the world and a view of God from which every missionary can begin teaching.[23]

Bear-Barnetson makes the application from the narrative of Acts that appropriate missionary practice is missing from much of contemporary effort in that there is a lack of appreciation and respect of the ancient culture of the recipients of the gospel message. She further describes the underlying spirituality in these cultures of origin and suggests that these cultural sources can serve as a foundation in which the gospel can be preached. This is distinct from merely a Native person desiring to garnish their worship services with the effects of their Native culture. This is speaking about a foundational preparation for gospel ministry that has been and still is ignored by non-Native missions to First Nations people.

Brown adds his comments regarding the Acts 17 passage.

God made us to be who he made us to be, and there aren't any mistakes. And that can be verified and clarified by Acts chapter 17, when Paul was talking to the men of Athens. And it tells them how all the people of the world will know him, and where many early people throughout the earth that had known this habitation that they live on was made by the hands of the one Great Spirit (not in a generic way) the one great Spirit that made all things, so they knew he was there, now they wanted to know how to get to him. And many did not know that God became a man.[24]

---

[23] Bear-Barnetson, 'Introduction to First Nations Ministry', p. 133.
[24] Brown, 'Telephone Interview with Larry "Grizz" Brown'.

With no desire to appear repetitious, I feel it is important to show, by these lengthy quotes, how articulate these ministers are in the ideas of redemptive analogy and their common understanding of the concept. Brown especially wants to point out that the Great Spirit is not a generic title for a god, but indeed is the Holy Spirit of God himself. This was a common belief I heard expressed in my research. Taylor contributes:

> And so when we're talking about contextualizing the gospel it's all about going into their communities, and utilizing what they already have in their culture that they believe the Creator gave them, and it's all based on the Acts and stuff and the examples of redemptive analogy.

> Well, I don't know if you heard what Paul was talking about, Paul was talking about between the history, four hundred years before while they were looking at this unknown god altar ... Then four hundred years after that there's only one of those altars standing up. And they are all doing devotions around it, and Paul talks to them and says, 'I want to remind you, I want to tell you who this unknown god is'. And so that's the redemptive analogy and the power of the redemptive analogy in that story. And what I do is, I go back to that Indian tribe and I talk to them using songs and I share with them, 'The God that you are singing about in your songs, do you know who he is? And why do you sing it to him?' And then, I declare to him who this unknown god is, and it is Jesus.[25]

Taylor is able to recount fully the extra-biblical tradition underlying the Mars Hill story. The importance of the ability to recount the redemptive analogy approach, for Taylor, is a missionary one. He uses, according to my interviews with him, this approach in all his outreaches, and prefers to call it 'common ground' type of evangelism. This follows Bear-Barnetson's methodology in using Paul as a model for doing missions and evangelism. This is important to my findings from the data. Contextualization for Native Americans is not about them feeling good about their background or exercising any kind of personal rights (although it is their God-given right to express their culture), but rather it stems from a desire to reach

---

[25] Taylor, 'Personal Interview'.

their elders and extended tribal family members with the life-giving message of the gospel of Jesus Christ. Taylor clearly is convinced that this Great Spirit, or unknown god, is indeed the third person of the Trinity, the Holy Spirit himself.

These comments from my interviewees concerning Acts 17 can find their hermeneutic in the one suggested by Richardson's book, *Eternity in Their Hearts*.[26] Richardson's explanation is fascinating in that it includes extra-biblical historical material to supplement Scripture. Taylor specifically refers to it as a 'redemptive analogy' and applies it to his usage of Pawnee language and culture.

Bear-Barnetson bases her 'Placement Theology' on Acts 17.

This conveys the idea that God supernaturally placed the people where He wanted them to be which correlates with the Apostle Paul's words in Acts 17:26, 'From one man he made every nation of men, that they should inhabit the whole earth; and He determined the times set for them and the exact places where they should live' ... The Creator placed them exactly where they live because He purposed and predestined places for them to live.

This leads to a discussion of the Divine purpose in the Divine placement of First Nations. Acts 17:27, 28 shed some light on the purposes that the Creator had in mind. 'God did this so men would seek Him and perhaps reach out for Him and find Him, though He is not far from each one of us. For in Him we live and move and have our being'.

It was the Creator's intention for First Nations people to understand Him through His attributes as revealed to them in the land. They then would reach out and love Him in return. The Creator was all around them, in their living, moving, and being. What was their 'living, moving, and being'? It was their environment and their culture.[27]

Bear-Barnetson here makes the connection between the placement of Native peoples upon the land and the gift of culture that the Creator gives, detailing the way culture becomes the initial way

---

[26] Richardson, *Eternity in Their Hearts*, pp. 9-71.
[27] Bear-Barnetson, 'Introduction to First Nations Ministry', p. 58.

that revelation is given. This is also a spatial understanding that is conducive to Native American ideas.

Acts 19

Bear-Barnetson goes on to point out that Paul does not speak against the gods of other religions, but rather uses their presence to point to the God above all others.

> In Acts 19, we find Paul getting into some trouble in Ephesus. Signs and wonders follow Paul's ministry and we even see people healed by cloths that had touched Paul. Then a silversmith named Demetrius (19:23) begins a riot against Paul. A great and angry crowd rushed Paul's companions into the theater where 'the whole city was in an uproar' (19:29). The main complaint Demetrius had was that his idol making business would be ruined and their god Artemis would not be worshipped.... It is astonishing that Paul escaped and did not blaspheme Artemis. In all of his preaching and teaching, Paul did not blaspheme the goddess of the Ephesians. He only spoke the truth about God and prayed for healing and deliverance for the people. The riot took place because many people had come to faith, not because Paul felt the need to denigrate their goddess in order to exalt Jesus.[28]

In this, it is clear that Native Americans are finding the Christianity they have needed that is in contrast to the prejudiced 'savage' approach to other religious people. This sets forth a missiology that is open to dialogue.

Acts 21

Here Bear-Barnetson speaks about Paul's participation in Jewish Purification Ceremonies. As a missionary on furlough, Paul fits back into his own culture and undergoes appropriate rituals commensurate with the expectations of those around him.

> In Acts 21, Paul arrives in Jerusalem. He tells James and all the elders the great news of the ministry among the Gentiles and they praise God, before informing Paul that ... thousands of Jews have believed, and all of them are zealous for the law. They have been informed that you teach all the Jews who live among

---

[28] Bear-Barnetson, 'Introduction to First Nations Ministry', p. 134.

the Gentiles to turn away from Moses, telling them not to cir-
cumcise their children or live according to our customs. 'What
shall we do?' (Acts 21:20-22) They immediately make plans to
prove to the Jews that Paul is '... living in obedience to the law'
(21:24). '(Paul) purified himself along with them. Then he went
to the temple to give notice of the date when the days of purification would end and the offering would be made for each of
them' (21:26) ... If one views Paul's partaking in purification
ceremonies through a missiological hermeneutic, one can per-
fectly understand him. In Acts, Paul was making a statement to
the Jewish believers. He was showing the Jews that he himself
was a Jew. He contextualized himself in order to be able to
preach the Gospel to his own people.[29]

As presented in Chapter 4, it is clear that for Bear-Barnetson,
smudging could be considered as such a purification ceremony or
ritual. It is a ceremony that adds primarily symbolic meaning to the
individual's faith until it is transformed in a Pentecostal way. But
like Paul in his home context, it is important for Native Americans
to relate to their own cultural context in ways that make sense to
those who subscribe to that culture and its religious symbols. In
this, she is building what Lingenfelter calls 'a new hermeneutic'.[30]

Other Dimensions

Other than the approach of Redemptive Analogy and Lukan Pentecostal Theology, I have witnessed and heard what I believe are five
dimensions of this Native American approach to contextualization.
These facets are not mentioned overtly by those that I interviewed
but are inherent in their comments precipitated by my line of ques-
tioning.

Subjectivity

The intrusion of white missionaries and anthropologists with their
outside perspective has made it desirable for Native Americans to
be able to make informed and formational decisions about the worship practices they employ. Indians do not want the white missionaries to continue making subjective judgments upon their religious
practices. In contrast, there is necessarily a protocol before non-

---

[29] Bear-Barnetson, 'Introduction to First Nations Ministry', p. 150.
[30] Lingenfelter, *Transforming Culture: A Challenge for Christian Mission*, p. 19.

Natives are allowed to experience Indian culture. Many Natives feel as one Seminole expressed to me, 'Not only do I not want you to come, I do not want you to see pictures of the observance, for everything that the white man has looked at he has ruined'. Fortunately for me, those whom I interviewed and the members of the churches I visited did not share such a strong aversion to my presence, nevertheless, the ceremonies are sacred enough to the people that they do not want interference. Those who would do Native ministry must take note.

Spirituality

Native Americans are one people group who are referred to as having a distinct spirituality in America. This term has become quite popular and now a theology of religions necessitates that cultural practices be approached from a spiritual perspective. This is facilitated by Pentecostal theology, which tends to approach things more in terms of Spirit, than merely in empirical ways. By this I mean that Pentecostalism features ways of knowing beyond mere rationality. Pentecostals do this (as do Native Americans, as demonstrated by Lundy's discernment) by starting with the Spirit, and emphasizing experience along with spiritual ways of knowing.[31]

Spatiality

The land, geography, and space are more important than history or documentary authority in Native worldview. Spatial concerns can be observed in the contextualization within the worship services, specifically in the materials used. These include:

- Local wood used in the construction of the drums as the myrtle wood at Sacred Ground Outreach in Siletz, Oregon;
- Sage (plant of this land) used to smudge the sick, instead of olive oil from Europe;
- Ceremonies and Dances that touch the earth;
- Talking Circles employing the passing of an eagle feather, a bird Native to this land.

In this time of great concern for ecology, Native Americans possess a theology that holds promise for the Church's renewed theology of

---

[31] Land, *Pentecostal Spirituality*, pp. 38-39; Lundy, 'Interview'.

space and place. In this area, Native Americans can make a great contribution.

Bear-Barnetson's Placement Theology

Bear-Barnetson talks about Native Americans basing their identity on where they originate, not where they presently live, or on their profession.[32] This idea of placement of people is an important dimension in everything they do. This is a part of the spatiality that is being called for in Native theology. When spatial concerns become more predominant in Native theologizing than temporal concerns, Native worldview will be more accurately understood.

Inter-tribalism

When I interviewed Barnetson, he was happy to talk about powwow and its meaning to contextual Natives in the movement.[33] The topic was inspired by my surprise at Barnetson's use of the word, 'Pan-Indian'. When asked, how do you feel about powwow? Barnetson answered;

> I think there are two things going on at the same time. One is a sense of survival purpose, and to fight against assimilation. If there's a move toward Pan-Indianism, there is also this retaining of tribal distinctive. They both have a value and they are not mutually exclusive, nor does one have to negate the other. They are two values that can both be embraced.

Barnetson agreed that the powwow movement, like other contextualized Native practice, was good vehicle to allow the gospel to be carried to Native peoples.[34]

The contemporary inter-tribal nature of the contextual movement is what may continue to cause the movement to grow, as it consolidates the commonalities of scattered tribes. The practice of contextualized ceremonies and the orality of the movement is more

---

[32] Bear-Barnetson, 'Introduction to First Nations Ministry', p. 55.

[33] The argument by some Assembly of God Natives that traditional practices should be avoided because powwow or pan-Indian practice is not authentic fails to recognize the important legitimacy of the powwow movement in Indian life (Tarango, '"Choosing the Jesus Way:" the Assemblies of God's Home Missions to American Indians and the Development of a Pentecostal Indian Identity', p. 167).

[34] Barnetson, 'Telephone Interview with Randy Barnetson'.

in keeping with the character of Native religion and its variation from the creed and dogma base of European Christianity. Dugan addresses this in her discussion of the Plains Indian.

> It is helpful to step for a moment outside the cultural experience of the Plains Indian to compare it with the experience of other Indian peoples on the American continent. Then the importance of the vision assumes its true proportions for the Plains dwellers. The existence of each tribe could be characterized as rather isolated, constituting a rounded and enclosed cosmos and having a cosmology of its own. This fact raises the question of the survival of its thought world. Would merely dogmatic statements be enough to guarantee the passing sown of an undiminished tradition? Is it sufficient to rely on the instillment of mythological stories and faithful observance of ritual to preserve the living spirit of a spiritual tradition?[35]

I conclude that the stories and rituals have indeed endured. This is clear as we observe the persistence of Indian culture despite a long history extending from well before the 'Trail of Tears' and including much of current colonial approaches to mission among these people from whom we have so much to learn. The participatory and tribal character is also part of what will make contextualized Indian Christianity a growing force during a post-modern age.

Benefits of Contextualization

The benefits of the contextual movement include a deepening of the spiritual worship of the local churches and a worldwide influence among indigenous peoples as well as others. This comes through a shift in Native American activity that focuses more on a thriving outreach that is centrifugal in nature, rather than an inward-turned focus that is centripetal.

Spiritual Worship
The positive spiritual effects of contextualized Native American worship were clear to me as I observed it as a Pentecostal minister. There was no sense of conflict within the services, and I observed

---

[35] Dugan, *The Vision Quest of the Plains Indians: Its Spiritual Significance*, pp. 171-72.

what I believed were traditional Indians taking part in the services. Though a few did not come forward to dance or be smudged, I felt that they intended to become more comfortable and more active in this different expression of the Christian faith.

Created Purpose

Taylor observes:

> It's not just because I can worship my God with the contemporary style, I love to. It's kind of like you can pray in your understanding and you can pray in tongues; it's something different. And that for me, that's the difference. I can worship God in another's man style and I can touch him, or I can worship him in the way that he created me to be.[36]

Native Americans who enjoy contextualizing their practices and ceremonies are not limited when they attend typical worship services with other cultures. It is a great benefit when they can worship in 'the Indian Way', for they feel more whole and there is a rightness about this cultural integration.

Ministry in a Good Way

The use of the word 'good' for Native peoples indicates something that is culturally appropriate and helpful. The word goes further in its indication of happiness, long life, and spiritual alignment with all of creation. The Navajo word *hozho* speaks of 'beauty, harmony, and happiness'.[37] This became clear to me in my visit to a disability agency in Flagstaff, Arizona, that contextualized practices to serve Native Americans. The name of the center was Hozhoni Foundation. So, in this context, I am speaking about a dimension of culturally appropriate practices in Christian ministry that are good for Native peoples and also good for the progress of their spiritual growth in the kingdom of God.

Worldwide Witness

Besides the great harvest reaped by the Window Rock Church of God through their contextualized Enemy Way Ceremony, I was impressed with Taylor's testimony of the missional power of contextualization. He recounts in detail:

---

[36] Taylor, 'Personal Interview'.
[37] Kidwell, Noley, and Tinker, *Native American Theology*, p. 109.

One time in Texas, in a Hispanic church, a bilingual church, they didn't know how it was going to work; neither did we, and we didn't really care. And so we just took some folks down there, and we were sitting in the night before Saturday night and some older Hispanic women were looking at me and stuff, and I said, 'What do you think about all this?' And they said, 'I don't know, I don't know'. And I said 'Don't you have any songs and stuff like that?' And they looked at me, and they got all embarrassed and I didn't know if I had broken some protocol with them and the lady that was there said, 'They're Mariachi'. And I said, 'What's that? Is that a curse word?' And she said 'No, they do Mariachi'. And I said, 'Mariachi!' And she said, 'No, cannot do in church, we are not allowed'. And I said, 'I'm the guest preacher and your pastor said I could do anything I wanted so you come with me, you wear Mariachi', and they begin to cry.

And so that morning I get up there, and there were like six or seven people in that church you know, all Hispanic you know. And we come in doing our dancing and we get up there and preach a little bit and I said, 'Okay, Mariachis you come up'. And here they came with their dresses in this huge stage, and I said, 'Well, sing one of your songs, not a Christian song, but one of your traditional songs'. And they start singing their songs and people didn't even have to tell. These old people began coming to the front. We didn't do an altar call, they just began coming up and the Hispanic pastor, an old and a very distinguished man was watching, and he began to dance and his wife began to dance and people began to cry, and I said, 'What are the words to this song?' And she began to cry, and she said, 'It means, Jesus loves you, John 3:16. They don't let us sing at church, because they don't know what it means. Mariachi is to be bad men'. So after that, you know, here's this Hispanic church and they want to reach their people using their culture. And here's all these Hispanic men down here, crying and weeping. And so contextualization transcends color, culture because it's scriptural. I mean Jesus and Paul were these great contextualizers.[38]

---

[38] Taylor, 'Personal Interview'.

This is an example of a Native Pentecostal preacher utilizing a contextual approach in an evangelistic outreach. Because the approach has a positive effect in Native experience, it can also be applied in other indigenous contexts. This clearly reveals a Native American minister's commitment to a contextualized form of evangelism and beautifully illustrates the power of Native practices to bring the lost into the light of the gospel.

Centripetal to Centrifugal

Native Americans in the past have attracted outsiders to their indigenous religion and practices by possessing a beautiful culture and spirit. Native American Pentecostals who are contextualizing their practices are working from the inside out as they reach out of a holistic center touching the world around them. It is not a new thing for Native peoples to enrich all that are around them, but their own expression of Pentecostal faith will avoid the white interference in a pure expression anointed by the Spirit of God. Rather than attracting outsiders (centripetal), the Great Commission will be fulfilled from the inside out (centrifugal) with a thoroughly integrated witness.[39]

Summary

The relevance of Native American contextualization for contemporary Native church life is complex. It serves as the basis for its significance while also promoting much controversy, as evidenced in the statements of the Christian and Missionary Alliance. The tremendous amount of assimilation that has taken place in churches makes the process difficult for untrained witnesses to sort out, especially if they are non-Indians. There is a similarity between the contemporary 'worship wars' among the Euro-American churches as they grapple with music styles and the Native American Churches dealing with the contextualization of traditional practices

There are wide ranging benefits that provide Native worshipers with a sense of rightness and Scriptural integrity in a cultural back-

---

[39] Richard Waldrop, 'Salvation History and the Mission of God: Implications for the Mission of the Church among Native Americans' (Paper presented at *The Missiology of Jamestown Consultation*, Regent University, Virginia Beach, Virginia, May 28-29, 2008), p. 15.

ground that is viewed mostly as neo-pagan at best by non-Natives. The Pentecostal churches I have observed contextualize certain practices and their members explain them in largely Pentecostal ways, integrated with a Native American approach that proves to be successful in local churches as well as international outreaches. The movement will only grow as it matures through theological training and multiplication of ministries, regardless of their denominational affiliation. In my recommendations, I will make direct application to one denomination, Church of God (Cleveland, TN), whose Native American members are increasingly identifying with the contextual movement.

6

CONCLUSIONS AND RECOMMENDATIONS

I will now turn to the conclusions and recommendations that have been prompted by my research and analysis of the various data. I will begin by revealing relevant findings and the ideas that were suggested by them. I further intend to follow those conclusions with suggestions for improvement in Native ministries, especially in organizations that locate themselves in the Pentecostal tradition.

Conclusions

The increasing presence of Native American traditional practices in Native American Pentecostal churches has brought great concern and prompted censure in the past due to fear of syncretism. The purpose of my study was to identify which practices are being contextualized and how these particular practices reduce syncretism. I conclude from the data, literary and qualitative, that there are a number of these practices, and that the use of these practices not only reduces syncretism because of the leadership of mature, biblically informed Native leaders, but provides numerous spiritual benefits for the Natives. In the development of the study, I identified the practices by analyzing the literature (Chapter 1) and by employing a methodology of qualitative research (Chapter 2), and concluded that there are six practices that were present in most, if not all contextual Native Pentecostal churches. They were language, smudging, drum and rattles, dance, talking circles, and ceremony.

These are not the only practices that Native Americans are contextualizing. One might find a Methodist pastor performing a pipe ceremony in a Presbyterian church, or a Pentecostal Native man who plays flute in the opening of every worship service. These six, however, were the practices that I observed among Native Pentecostals or were referred to by them in interviews. The contextual movement is certainly larger than the Pentecostal faith, but as noted in my delimitations, my focus has been on Pentecostalism so that I can demonstrate how the significance of my research applies to my own denomination.

I realized my purpose, as I initially set out to see if there are contextual Native Pentecostal churches. I discovered not only that there are, but, in fact there are few contextual churches that are not in some way, connected to Pentecostalism. This was a significant finding. I further realized my purpose by collecting data, both literary and qualitative. I analyzed the data through thematic coding that gave me the important ways and categories that enabled the Natives to reduce syncretism by utilizing their own internal model of critical contextualization. My interviews confirmed that the leaders were familiar with Hiebert's model and had modified it to suit their context by integrating their practices with their particular approaches. This became the outline I followed for each practice in Chapter 3. It has been a humbling experience to attempt to critique or add to the work of the late Paul G. Hiebert. I only pray that the reader understands that coupled with any critiques I might make is a deep gratitude for the man and his theories.

My analysis of both the literary and qualitative data yielded relevant findings that described exactly why this contextual behavior is both beneficial and important for Native Americans. Beyond the continuity it provides by integrating Native worldview into Christian practice, there are a host of other important symbols, functions, and spiritually transformative experiences that this behavior brings to their worship. The Native Pentecostals also pointed to how contextualization strengthens their evangelistic and missional activities, helping me to realize my goal of enabling them to proceed with an integrated witness by describing in their own words how they are reaching the world with the traditions given to them by the Creator. I use the word 'enable' lightly, because Native ministries have been reaching the world long before I ever considered undertaking this research. My objective, however, was to give my interviewees 'a voice', to enable others to hear them and recognize the thought that they give to the relevance of their ancient practices in the context of contemporary worship

Given that a discussion already exists in their periodical and monographic literature, it has been important for me to cite that literature and include quotes from it in my work. Clearly, Native Americans desire to contextualize practices (even resulting in formal statements from the movement), and I must demonstrate that here in order to be faithful to them and to my goal in doing this research. Their research and my work closely correlate with the process I observed in the descriptive interviews. Giving voice to this discussion and concluding that there are at least three levels in their active results of contextualization in the worship services enabled me to describe the relevance through anthropological, theological, and missiological reflection. The findings revealed the particular ways in which they go about including the practices in their services and evangelistic endeavors. My findings revealed that the way in which contemporary North American Indians are contextualizing the practices is through a combination of a modified model of critical contextualization that draws upon Richardson's concept of redemptive analogy, as well as demonstrates a clear understanding of both Kraft's and Hiebert's principles of contextualization. This is resulting in a Native American Lukan Pentecostal hermeneutic that is continuing to develop and will, no doubt, have considerable impact on the changing face of indigenous worship. It is my belief that Cheryl Bear-Barnetson's biblical section of her dissertation reflects the future paradigm for Native Pentecostal theological analysis. Building on Richardson and utilizing the Acts narrative, Bear-Barnetson makes her approach doubly effective by suggesting a segue for a narrative theology that legitimizes contextualization of Native American practices by following the missionary practices of the Apostle Paul. Though this theology is yet to be built in any formal way, I present it as a wave of the future and look forward to seeing others follow in her footsteps.

Also in my findings is the discovery that numerous benefits have resulted from the use of contextual practice. This was the essence of Chapters 4 and 5. That Native Americans have their own distinct ways of doing church has never been in question, but due to widespread suspicion and fear it has been oppressed and repressed. Contextual Native Americans enjoy sharing their cultural richness with many indigenous peoples across the globe, and hopefully, through encouragement reinforced with studies such as mine, these 'prophets can be honored in their own country'.

Having realized my purpose and goal through relevant findings, I hope to make a significant contribution to my own denomination's Indian ministries by making valid recommendations for future initiatives. The progress toward encouraging contextual Native Pentecostal churches that took place under the leadership of Paul Risser in the Foursquare Church encouraged my hope for the Church of God (Cleveland, TN) and any other group that desired to extend Native ministries in this fashion. Although the Foursquare eventually rescinded some of the positive moves, there is, according to my research, still a significant amount of good will in their denomination toward reaching all expressions of Native American Christians.

My denomination (Church of God-Cleveland, TN) needs to engage the future of Native Ministries. Church leaders often are bewildered and ignorant as to how to proceed. One desire of my heart is to provide much needed information to help end the ignorance, fear, and prejudice.

The results of my study were never intended merely to tell the Native Pentecostals what they are doing, or just to add to the growing corpus of literature on Native American contextualization. I am now able, as a result of my findings, to make valid informed recommendations to my denomination – informative enough, that if taken seriously, could remove the fear and prejudice that leads to prohibitions that impede missionary progress and growth of the churches in Indian country.

There has been much damage done in the area of Native American missions by non-Native leaders. I have come to see the problem as similar to a love relationship between a man and woman, one having done so much damage to the relationship that it is beyond repair. No matter how much they, or others, feel that it is right for them to be together, they must part. While Natives and non-Natives celebrate their oneness in the body of Christ, I do not believe non-Natives can lead Native American ministry any longer, no matter how pious or well informed the leader may be.

I have already experienced the suspicion of non-Native church leaders in discussing my research with them. Yet, I have felt it has been a worthy effort. Love works, whether it believes it can repair the breech or not. I love the Indians I have met and sat with. They have been kind to me. While my study may not have repaired anything, I pray that the time, energy, and money spent will rise as incense to the Great Holy Spirit, who is worthy of all praise.

Recommendations for Transforming Praxis

The following recommendations correlate essentially with my questions. I began by asking 'In what ways does contextualizing traditional practices enhance worship?' My answers prompt certain *practical* recommendations. These are recommendations that pertain to the necessity of allowing Native Pentecostal leaders to exercise leadership in what is included in the worship services.

My second question pertained to the issue of whether or not contextualization is beneficial to aid the Native Pentecostals' spiritual worship or success in worldwide evangelism and witness. The answers that the study produced demonstrate the great need for specific *structural* recommendations for denominations and/or organizations. My intent at this juncture in the process is to detail these recommendations by encouraging a transformation of *praxis*.[1]

Transforming Praxis

Native Americans are developing a transformed praxis in their worship services. There must also be an accompanying, intentional transformed praxis in church life to ensure that this move continues. It must continue because, as my research demonstrates, it is beneficial for the people. The non-Natives have much to learn and receive from Native people in regard to discovering a spirituality that is true both to our neighbors and to the land upon which we live.

Freedom of Expression

During the time of this study, it was brought to my attention that a beloved non-Native missionary who was well-respected by both me and my denomination, was giving slide presentations during speaking engagements, warning in tears against what is called for by my dissertation. She represents a large number of non-Native mission-

---

[1] Praxis is here defined as 'practice, as distinguished from theory'.

aries, still faithfully serving on reservations, that feel that Native American contextualization is a dangerous move back to the past and closer toward neo-paganism. While there is no need for those who do not wish to participate in these practices to do so, nor for anyone to violate his or her conscience in this regard, there must be an admonition by the leadership of the churches that those who *do* desire to practice them to be permitted to do so.

Pentecostal churches have come a long way in undoing the legalistic prohibitions of the Holiness movement, sometimes even to the extreme of falling into the opposite trap of permissiveness. In the last thirty years, the Pentecostal movement has been able to move beyond the areas of dress and behavior to include worship styles such as creative movement, drama, and contemporary music. While there are still cultural battles being fought, the war is largely won. It must be bewildering for Native Americans to witness the use of multiplied drums and percussion instruments in non-Native worship, having had their singular drum previously outlawed!

The multiplication of districts successfully implemented by the Foursquare Church (which I will consider further in my section on structural recommendations) has proven helpful in Pentecostal organizations, not only in adding indigenous leadership and giving more direct supervision to indigenous churches, but also in providing a 'buffer' zone where cultural incompatibility exists. I recall a conversation with a denominational mission official who described to me how in Central America those who desired to contextualize Mayan cultural practices found it easier to worship in a separate district from those neighbors who felt they were in error. The two groups were able to worship together in the larger assemblies, but preferred to express their faith locally in a way that was more conducive to their Indian culture.

This type of practical approach allows for freedom of expression until ignorance and prejudice can be dealt with. The Azusa Centennial included contextualized Pentecostal worship in the services and venue, but few expressions of such from 'language churches' or those that might include traditional practices. After the services, I observed Native Americans in regalia in the restaurants eating on one side of the building and those in suits and ties on the other – a reflection, perhaps, of the propensity of one group to dominate the others in the larger assemblies, rather than collaborate as equals in worship and fellowship.

While we will never fully remove the differences of expression, and it is not my place to do so, there must be no invasions, impositions, or prohibitions on those congregations whose pastors desire to include traditional practices, such as was endured by the congregation at Window Rock, Arizona.

Sensitivity Training

One would not think that the church that serves the God of love would need the same type of instruction that care providers receive. One would guess it would come part and parcel with the sacrificial love that accompanies salvation. This assumption is part of what has gotten us to this place. One would even imagine that missionary training would be sufficient to prepare the outsiders to love the insiders. As I have demonstrated in this study, the history of Christian missions among Native Americans has been tainted by compromise with the government, cultural ignorance, paternalism, and ultimately violence. It is for this reason that a whole new orientation must take place in the churches. This needful sensitivity training, coupled with better history classes in our schools telling the whole story of the eradication of Indian tribes, would need to include material such as found in Woodley and Twiss.[2] These works are helpful in that they are not just an attempt to spread 'political correctness', but are theological works written by leaders of the church who understand the situation and are themselves pastors.

Native Ministry Training

Even in contexts where there are non-Natives pastoring Native American congregations, there must be Native scholars teaching ministers and leaders. While empowering Native leaders to reach the harvest, we must also be trained by the people themselves to minister in an inter-cultural fashion appropriate to Native American hearts and minds.

Transformational Structures

Along with attitude and educational changes that allow for the free cultural expressions of the people we are trying to reach, there must

---

[2] Woodley, *Living in Color*; Twiss, *One Church Many Tribes*.

also be corresponding adjustments to prepare the wineskin of the Church to receive the new wine that God is giving. The following recommendations are intended to apply to the present Indian ministries of the Church of God (Cleveland, TN).

Indigenous Leadership

Both Four Winds and Southwest Indian Ministries are led by non-Natives. This is a situation that perpetuates two age-old problems: (1) a lack of indigenous leadership, and (2) the continuing self-defeating belief that Native Americans are a perpetual mission field. Though admirable steps have been made in these ministries, a need still exists after all these years for indigenous leadership among American Indians. Much of what I have called for in the previous section could be corrected for the most part by appointing indigenous leaders for the following reasons: (1) indigenous leaders would help to provide understanding of the cultural practices; (2) trust would be established with the people that would build cooperation; and (3) the need for cultural training would be reduced, although not eliminated.

Native Districts Distinct From Multi-Cultural Ministry

It is my understanding that all other Indian churches in our denomination report to their respective state or regional office and that each have a state representative that presents their needs to their leadership. This is inadequate in the respect that there few opportunities for inter-tribal gatherings. The Southwest Indian Ministries has their own separate camp meeting and there is little or no interaction with the Native churches in other areas of the country. In the Foursquare Church that I observed, the Native districts work well and empower the people.

A Model for the Future Native American Leadership of the Church of God

While Paul Risser and his colleagues multiplied regional 'districts' for Foursquare Churches across the United States and Canada, a different thing was happening to the First Nations and Native peoples.[3] They were actually uniting tribes from different localities into a unit or district that was distinctly Native. This restructuring actu-

---

[3] Paul Risser, 'Telephone Interview with Paul Risser' (2008).

ally followed a model found in Indian country. There has been a social phenomenon since the World Wars that finds relationship in the recent contextual movement: the powwow. While some anthropologists brand the powwow as just another step to assimilation, the dances, drums, and other cultural expressions give common ground to various tribes who come together for gatherings. While Bear-Barnetson states that some of the dances that are done are 'owned' by different tribes, many are common and shared across tribal lines.

This suggests that an inter-tribal state or district could be established in the Church of God to gather the scattered Native churches. There will be some opposition to this, because many tribes, with their distinct creation myths and titles such as 'the Principal People', will not be interested in actually gathering and sharing leadership with other tribes. Also to be considered is the reality that many Native Pentecostals who were assimilated culturally into white culture (many forcibly) or oppose contextualization for their own theological reasons, will and do show displeasure with the contextual movement, saying they 'left all that in Egypt'. There is also, in Indian Country, an idea that Native Americans live in two worlds, and that there is no reason to contextualize traditional practices, but merely live the church life and the tribal life separately.[4] Still all in all, the gatherings I have observed, many of which are led by Foursquare Natives, are inter-tribal in character.

In noting the recent changes and successes within the Foursquare Church, I want to acknowledge that Bear-Barnetson is a woman and the highest leader in the First Nations Unit of Canada. Although I've not addressed the issue of women in leadership in this dissertation, it is my hope that future dialogues with the Foursquare Church will have a motivational effect upon the Church of God regarding women in ministry. Bear-Barnetson was, at the time of her appointment, the only First Nations licensed minister in the Foursquare Canada unit. Women have been the only ones doing ministry in many contexts of the Church of God, but have not

---

[4] Following Hiebert, Shaw, and Tienou, *Understanding Folk Religion*, p. 15. This is a sure way of ensuring syncretism, or what he calls 'dual religion'. This would enable Native Americans to follow their own practices in Indian contexts and Christian practices in Church. By doing so, never the twain shall meet, thereby removing the impetus for contextualization and cultural relevance of Christianity in the Native environment. This is not what I have described.

been treated equally. I have gained much inspiration and insight from the Natives' descriptions of their own understanding and practice of leadership.

Change Action Plan For Church of God Indian Ministries

I know of no church leader who has effected more change in a single organization than Hans Finzel. The change strategy I set forth below for the Church of God is inspired by and roughly based on the outline of his plan as set forth in *Change is Like a Slinky*.[5]

1. Accept the fact that our Indian Ministries have failed to reach the harvest. In dialogue with traditional Natives, acknowledge the failure of white missions. Distribute this work as introductory information. This step is not intended to suggest that whites and other cultures will ever be able to comprehend all the nuances of American Indians, but is intended to be a moral step of love and understanding as peoples throughout the body of Christ seek to unite with one another through mutual respect.

2. Acknowledge that the North American Indian Contextual Movement is an important movement in the future of Indian ministry. Invite contextual ministries to minister in our churches. Insure that denominational leaders support contextual Indian gatherings. Distribute articles from reputable periodicals such as *Christianity Today*.

Not all Indians will begin contextualizing practices, playing drums or dancing in regalia. An embrace of those that do contextualize will lead to a deeper understanding of and respect for the culture. Christians in North America need to celebrate the beauty and rich cultural diversities of our wonderful land.

3. Anticipate that many established Indian churches and leaders might resist this as syncretism. Leaders should not be defensive. It may be necessary to work separately with those who contextualize and with those who do not contextualize for a certain period of time. Leaders should anticipate the support of many independents and Foursquare Natives. Meet with Foursquare leaders and listen with open minds and hearts to the stories detailing the challenges of instituting Native districts.

---

[5] Hans Finzel, *Change Is Like a Slinky* (Northfield, VT: Northfield Publishing, 2004).

4. Follow through with a plan that is an improvement on the failed mission history. The work we have done since 1603 has yielded only a two to three percent harvest of those won to Christ. A contextualized approach will be more effective. We must move with confidence as we witness groups like the Foursquare having successes in Native ministry. Native leaders who are attending the contextual movement meetings underground must be encouraged that they are valued and a part of the greater whole.

5. Adjust our course as we listen and learn from Natives in the talking circles. At this juncture, the prophetic words of Vine Deloria should be recalled:

> Years ago, churches, anthropologists, and bureaucrats all discovered it was a good idea to have Indians attend a meeting on Indian problems. It looked better. But they certainly didn't have to invite the wrong kind of Indian. Like the treaty-makers of old, they could pick and choose who would represent the tribe and what philosophy he would support. Red Leaders therefore had to adopt an official double-talk in order to bring reservation problems into the sphere of national communication.[6]

It will be necessary, as all white leaders witness this new approach, to be prepared to accept the 'mavericks' who hold significant influence in the new spirit movements such as the contextual movement and remember that they can save the organization from institutionalism and 'bring us the future', even with 'messes'.[7]

6. Leaders should align Native ministries teams as they facilitate the course of change by endeavoring to unite those who contextualize with traditional church Native peoples. Risser and the Foursquare leaders implemented the following steps, and they are most appropriate:

- Ask the Native people what they want, instead of acting on their behalf.
- Listen and honor the Native People.
- Give them their own district.

---

[6] Deloria, *Custer Died for Your Sins: An Indian Manifesto*, p. 207.
[7] H. Finzel, *Top Ten Mistakes Leaders Make* (Colorado Springs, CO: Cook Communications Ministries International, 2000), p. 73.

- Plant indigenous churches.
- Release Native leadership.
- At the appropriate time, appoint a Native leader over newly united Inter-tribal Indian Ministries.

It may be necessary to dissolve Southwest Indian Ministries; or, at the very least, a Native leader must be appointed over it. There will be a need to develop more decentralized leadership structures under Native leaders. Today, Southwest Indian Ministries, head-quartered in Gallup, New Mexico, has dozens of churches among the Navajo and Zuni, and is an organized department under the umbrella of the Church of God USA Missions. A full-time director, who answers to a board, leads this ministry. Certainly, Indian ministries should be taken out from under the wing of the USA Missions Department; this will remove the implication that they are a perpetual mission field. They should be organized as their own territory (much the same as denominational Hispanic territories) with indigenous leaders.

Final Words

The conclusions I have reached in the course of this research necessitate changes in attitude, changes in approach that are past due, and a plan for a restructuring of leadership applied to one Pentecostal denomination. I conclude with several recommendations that include a model for the future Native American leadership of the Church of God, and an action plan for change for Church of God Indian ministries. It is evident that a culturally appropriate approach to Indian ministries involves a degree of release and trust, with no restrictions motivated by fear and prejudice. The Native American leaders in our communities are not children; indeed, many are Bible college and seminary trained, seasoned pastors, capable of exercising spiritually discerning oversight over the remote congregations of our continent.

A number of Church of God members and leaders are already attending contextual movement events, but do so more or less underground. This is unhealthy and promotes the kind of 'split-level Christianity' that has been characteristic of the modern period. In this study I have detailed both a way of understanding and a way forward as demonstrated by a sister denomination. Fear and prejudice is based on ignorance. King said, 'There is little hope for us until we become tough-minded enough to break loose from the shackles of prejudice, half-truths and downright ignorance. The shape of the world today does not permit us the luxury of soft-mindedness'.[8]

Fear and prejudice toward contextual efforts must be removed through open minded prayerful reflection as Native leaders are encouraged to discern their own communities and practices. It is time for white leaders to stop acting on behalf of Native people. Denominational and organizational leadership must allow Native American worldviews to be widely shared through publications, and Native ministerial training that is both by and for Natives must be empowered.

In the introduction, I quoted E. Stanley Jones' call for renewed trust. This trust will be the tough work of the non-Natives in the denomination. The discernment and contextualization can be done by the Native leaders themselves, so that is not a task for us to have to comprehend entirely. The work of the denominations who are blessed with Native American and First Nation members is a moral work and one that only trust and God's love can produce. To put it another way, the words of John V. Taylor are similar: 'Are we of the West prepared to trust the Holy Spirit to lead the Christians of Asia and Africa, or must a controlling Western hand be permanently resting on the Ark of God?'[9] God grant the Church the love and trust to avoid the death trap of Hophni and Phineas, to take our hand off the work of the Spirit and rejoice in the movements of new life that God is granting the Church.

---

[8] M.L. King, *Strength to Love* (Minneapolis, MN: Fortress Press, 1982), p. 17.

[9] J.V. Taylor, *The Primal Vision: Christian Presence Amid African Religion* (Minneapolis, MN: Fortress Press, 1963), p. 9.

Appendix A

Navajo Enemy Way Ceremony

By Johnson Dennison[1]

The Navajo Enemy Way Ceremony is a healing ceremony to treat patients and is only conducted in the summer months. This ceremony is almost a week-long process for patients who are ill from any form of illness. It was originally conducted for individuals who participated in a foreign war and usually for warriors returning from war. This is why it is called the Nidaa', the Enemy Way Ceremony. Some people call it a 'Squaw dance', but that is derogatory.

The preparation for the Enemy Way Ceremony begins by building a forked stick hogan. It can also be conducted in any type of traditional hogan as well. Most of the time, a temporary hogan-shaped brush arbor is built for the ceremony. The temporary shelter is dismantled as soon as the ceremony is over. Another small arbor is built in front of the hogan, also for a ceremonial purpose.

A larger arbor is also built about fifty yards from the hogan on the southwest side. This is to be used as a cook shed where visitors are received and are fed. The relatives of the patients will help build the cook shed. The shed is usually divided into two rooms. The room on the north side is reserved for the main patient and his family to prepare food for the visitors. The south room is reserved for the wife of the patient and her family to use for receiving friends and relatives.

---

[1] Johnson Dennison, 'Spiritual Perspectives: The Navajo Enemy Way Ceremony', *Gallup Independent* (Web Edition) June 25, 2005.

The patients will invite their clan relatives and friends to the Enemy Way ceremony. It is a major Navajo ceremony involving a lot of people from communities. It is also a public ceremony, so anyone can attend.

There is a meeting night to start the ceremony. Most of the relatives and friends of the patients will come to the meeting night. It is usually on a Monday. The visitors and relatives will come into the hogan and make donations. Because the hogan is small and not everyone will fit, there will be some people standing outside. The people will talk about the ceremonial process and at the same time they will discuss who will receive the ceremonial staff.

A ceremonial staff is a foot and a half long cut-off cedar juniper branch decorated with eagle feathers and colorful yarn. The ceremonial staff is obtained and decorated on the day when it will be carried to the receiver. The receiver of the staff will eventually be considered as the person to treat the patients. The patients and visitors will decide who will receive the staff. The meeting night is concluded in the late evening while singers sing sacred songs of the Enemy Way ceremony as they stand in front of the hogan facing east.

Most of the people will leave and go home for the night, except the patients and their family members, who will camp out for the night. Throughout the evening, a reception is provided at the cook shed for the visitors. The main dish is usually mutton stew, roast mutton, with coffee, and fry bread.

It is also a time to socialize and exchange stories and greetings. Most of the people also bring some food with them to help out the family. The ceremony is well announced through a Navajo radio station to which every one listens daily, so it is not a surprise event for people.

The next morning at dawn, the spokesperson with the patients will drive over to the staff receiver's house or hogan to make an offering. Long ago, it was one person to ride a horse a distance to meet the staff receiver. The person to receive the staff usually does not live in the same community as the main ceremonial camp.

When they, patients and spokesperson, arrive at the staff receiver's house, they will offer him the collection of donations, so he will serve the patients as a medicine man. Generally, he will agree to receive the staff. Sometimes he may refuse to receive the sacred staff for several reasons. To receive a staff is a huge responsibility. However, when he agrees, he will set a date to receive the staff. He will announce by saying when the staff should be brought to him.

The elders tell us that a long time ago people used to announce five days to seven days. But nobody does that anymore. If more than three days is announced, the Enemy Way ceremony will last more than a week or even two weeks. The even number of days are not considered; it has to be an odd number. Three day agreements are most common in Enemy Way ceremonies.

The Navajo people always predict it will be three days to carry the staff, so they schedule a planning meeting on Monday night. A proposal is made on Tuesday morning, and three days after Tuesday is Friday. The day the staff is carried over is usually on Friday, so it will become a weekend activity. The day would finally arrive at the ceremony to fix, decorate, and carry the staff to the staff receiver's hogan. Usually a crowd gathers to participate. A number of people ride their horses or bring their horses in stock trailers. While waiting for the afternoon ceremony to start, visitors are received at the cook shed and meals are served. Inside the hogan, people have already brought colorful yarn to be used in decorating the staff, horses, and even vehicles. Another selected medicine man will bring in a straight cut off juniper branch, well prepared to be decorated for a sacred staff. The medicine man will sing sacred songs while decorating the staff. A design is inscribed on the staff and colorfully decorated with yarn, eagle feathers and deer hooves. The patients and relatives pray while making the offering of corn pollen. It is a dramatic ritual activity.

When it is done, the main patient takes the staff outside and gets on a saddled horse. He takes off with the rest of the riders. There would be a number of horseback riders joining the patient carrying the staff. The rest of the people that don't have horses will follow the riders in their vehicles. This is a spectacular sight to see on the Navajo Reservation roads in the summer: a convoy of trucks and cars decorated with colorful yarn.

The horseback riders will arrive at the hogan of the person to receive the decorated staff. The main patient gets off his horse and comes into the hogan of the staff receiver while carrying the staff. He, the patient, will hand the staff over to the staff receiver while he is sitting on a buckskin in the hogan. The staff is well inspected by the receiver and his helper(s) to see if it was properly prepared. A medicine man will sing a receiving song. Following this, the traditional food is served to all people that came from the main camp of the ceremony. There will be greetings between family members, relatives, and friends from both camps as well. The family members of the receiver are the host.

In the late evening, the staff receiver and his helpers will start singing Enemy Way songs. The dancing starts next. A young girl dressed in traditional attire will come out of the hogan and initiate the dances. It is an activity many Navajo people like to participate in.

The next day is when the main patient and his family and relatives are served breakfast. After breakfast, the main patient and his family members will come to the front of the hogan and sing more sacred songs. While they are singing, they will be given gifts. After the singing is done, the main patient and family members will go home for the day. They will arrive back at the main camp at mid-morning. There will be visitors coming throughout the day and having a feast at the cook shed.

Late afternoon, the staff receiver, his family, and relatives will set up camp to spend the night about three miles from the main ceremonial camp. This is the time when more people will also join the dancing, called 'round dancing'. They will camp out along the side of the road. This type of camp is usually visible from the road. The Navajo people called it a 'camp out' and some called it 'second night'.

The next morning when the sun rises, the campers will move to the main camp of the ceremony. When they arrive, the horseback riders will ride back and forth between the main camp hogan and the staff receivers on horseback. The patients are all sitting in the hogan. As soon as the staff receiver arrives, the people from the main camp will serve breakfast.

But the staff receiver and his people still camp about a hundred yards away from the main camp. After breakfast, the people from the staff receiver's camp will come to the front of the main hogan and sing more sacred songs. As they sing, they will be given gifts from the main patient and his family members. Another medicine man specialized in the Enemy Way ceremony will conduct a ceremony most of the morning inside the hogan. The patients will spend most of morning in the hogan.

The spouse of the main patient will also participate in the ceremony, but under the small shade especially built for her just outside of the hogan. This is the time that she will be dressed with shawls, robes, fabric materials, and buckskin. She will take all these materials back to her family and relatives and they receive them as gifts from the main patient. This is considered as a main event of the ceremony.

Following the main events, there will be more round dancing. The final night of the ceremony is usually quiet, and very few people will stay as most of the people will be too tired to do anymore singing and dancing. The staff receiver stays until dawn the next morning. There will be some more closing songs sung at this time. The Enemy Way ceremony is over.

The sun rises, everything is quiet, and everyone gets to live normal lives again. The total process lasts six days. Again, the Navajo radio stations will start announcing more upcoming Nidaa' ceremonies. This is a Navajo cultural and ritual healing ceremony. The culture is still strong out in the Navajo country.

APPENDIX B

THE CONTEXTUALIZED ENEMY WAY CEREMONY

By Pastor Jerry Tom, Window Rock Church of God[1]

So the squaw dance is the enemy way; years ago the enemy would come and take over and people would be shot or injured or they would go to war. Sometimes there would be a psychological reaction in the mind, it's like today having the post-trauma stress syndrome and because of that people go to relapse, they go back to Vietnam, and it's like a backfire (this might be another term for 'flashback'). And they go back and sit there and their mind is not with them so men years ago would go to the council or years back we used to have a believer as our president, and then one of our staff, he wasn't a believer but he worked for him, and he went to Vietnam, and because of that he had all these blackouts and backfires. And his wife left him because he was too violent, he would wake up choking his wife, getting mean and he would get involved in alcohol, drinking and all that, and he went to psychiatrists and all of that and then he went to the medicine man and told him what was going on, and the medicine man told him; 'I know what's wrong with you, you see, your mind and your soul is still at Vietnam, so we need to bring those two back together'. So he recommended a squaw dance.

A squaw dance is sort of like a replica of war, you see what it does is; there are three ways, first they have a bundle, it's like a stick

---

[1] Tom and Harvey, 'Window Rock Church of God Interview'.

and it has all kinds of ribbons and strings and it's all done by prayer and singing and they all come together, and there is a patient, maybe he is someone that had post-traumatic stress syndrome. And he was there, and they did all that stuff and they did this thing where you ride a horse and they go out, and maybe about ten miles away there's destination, what it does is that those ten miles from 'a' to 'b' it's like war, they are going after the enemy. Going after whatever it is that got you, whatever it is that got your mind and soul. So it's more like a spiritual war than a physical one so the whole 'ride a horse' is more like a metaphor. Also years ago they used to go with guns and everything, ready to go to war so when they reached their destination they would shoot up in the air. And then they would get off of the horses and they would sing and they would pray. And they would bring back a skull representing that the enemy had been captured.

Another way would be that they would go from 'a to b to c' and there would be one night in between. So they would bring up that prisoner, that spirit, that thing. And it would cause some to go insane or it would cause problems, and when they would come back, there would be a celebration. They would celebrate capturing that thing that made this man go crazy, and so there would be a celebration. The men would all come together and sing and would have this big bonfire and then the women would come and choose the men and then danced with them. And so that second night they would do all that and then they would sing towards one another and they would make fun of one another, and it's sort of happy songs. But the next day that would be the third day, they would come back to the place where they started.

Usually Sunday morning, they would come back with the enemy captured. And then they would go inside, and there would be prayer. And they would take him out of that place, and they would patiently pray for him, and then they would come back inside. And he went through all that, and then the third day he was healed. Nothing ever happened again, no relapses, no backfires, nothing. So then he would come back and they would have a celebration again, and they would bring all these candy and stuff. Because he has come home, that man has come home. Also we used to have a camp meeting, we had the wagons tied to the horses, maybe two miles away from where we were. And then we would ride the wagons and the horses all wearing jewelry, and then we would go where the church used to be. And we were over there and we just felt because it was a revival, so then they would have food and candy, so now, this is no longer tradition, we got away from that now we are celebrating for Jesus Christ.

One of the things wrong with the churches here in the Navajo Nation; is that it never compares with the traditional Squaw Dance. In their dances, they bring a thousand dollars, they give truckloads of wood to cook in, they bring in water and sheep like so and so is having a squaw dance. That's all it is about now, and then they go to the clan, and the talk on the radio about certain clans, they say; 'this is your father' or 'this is your brother', they belong to the same clan even though they live twenty miles away and they don't even know it, but because they are in the same clan, it gives people permission to draw them together. So what it does is it draws people together, and it bring alcohol, there's fighting, sometimes they even kill one another. It goes so overboard that it's no longer sacred, but the churches do not believe that, they think that it doesn't happen that way and when they ask for sheep, nobody gives one, and this is Navajo, this is culture for us and yet, nobody wants to give the sheep. And one time I went to this place fifty miles away from here where they were having a squaw dance. And I saw all these sheep skins that had been given to that dance group for the people to eat, so I started counting and found thirty two sheep skins, thirty two ... and it's all free, it was given. It's not so much an offering, it is giving to the people, it is a gathering of clans, of relatives, and that makes them strong.

So wherever you go; whether it is a council meeting, a group meeting, when an elder talks, he will start off by saying; 'I am from this clan, these are my grandparents, they are from ...' and all that kind of stuff and then he calls to the people to put their guards down and honor them. And then he begins to talk, and that kind of thing is what brings us together, and that's why I think the Navajos are strong together, because they are clans.

See, a Navajo can leave the reservation, but the reservation never leaves his heart. He always comes back, because this kind of thing is underneath; we are friends, we are together, we're one people. And this is God moving now; this is God moving on the people. We've got some churches together, some white churches, Mex-

ican churches, Navajo churches all together. And we all got together and got on horseback, and went to Gallup Canyon, God was
moving in an incredible way. And we also did the same thing, we
brought some sheep, we asked people for sheep and they gave
them to us. And after the church services every night we would
make announcements, we would say; 'Before you go home, there's
some free food for you, you can go home and eat it. Or eat it here
with us and then tell all your relatives to come for the free food.
Instead of having sandwiches cut in half like the white folks, but we
have traditional Navajo food, people get in line, and they can eat as
much as they want to. So here the whole thing changes, there is no
alcohol, no fights; it's just people coming together, blacks, whites,
Mexicans, and Navajos coming together. And that is what it's all
about.

Well, we had a pastor that dressed very traditionally because he
was a silversmith; he made his own bracelets and all of that. So he
dressed really traditional, he even wore one of those hats that the
elders wore, which the Christian thinks that he is the medicine man,
but he's the one that holds the whole thing together. Yeah, he is a
pastor, he runs the whole thing, so when all the pastors would
come together and we would eat and we would have all of our ladies together, and we stayed at the campground all week and never
went home. We stayed there, and wake up in the morning to cook
for the pastors. Most important in there being underneath was being the pastor. Yeah, every year in different places, and it got bigger
and bigger and bigger each year, at one point we had a 100 by 150
foot tent and filled it up with more than a 1,000 people. Over the
years maybe about 30,000, or 20,000 came to Jesus, so we made an
impact. And one thing we used to do; it was that we would do a
give-away I mean people would gather after the squaw dance and
they would give out, to the people. And so we grabbed on to that
concept, we would give away cases of pops, Crackerjacks, candy,
materials ... to the ladies flowers and coffee ...

Appendix C

Participant Observations

Participant Observation	Location	Date of Service
Azusa Centennial Native American Gathering	Los Angeles, California	April 25-28, 2006
Eagle Butte Church of God	Eagle Butte, South Dakota	June 25, 2006
First Nations Foursquare Church	Santa Fe Springs, California	June 17, 2007
Window Rock Church of God	Window Rock, Arizona	May 27, 2008
Ordination Service	East Ridge, Tennessee	November 16, 2008
Bacone College Chapel	Muskogee, Oklahoma	February 17, 2009
Sacred Ground Outreach	Siletz, Oregon	March 29, 2009
Cherokee Church of God	Cherokee, North Carolina	April 5, 2009
Apple Valley Foursquare Church	Apple Valley, California	June 14, 2009

APPENDIX D

PERSONAL INTERVIEWS

Personal Interview	Location	Topics
Randy Barnetson June 17, 2007	Santa Fe Springs, California	smudging
Randy Barnetson August 9-10, 2007	Telephone interview	pow wow, smudging, talking circles
Larry 'Grizz' Brown November 19, 2007	Telephone interview	drum, contextualization
Jerry Tom, Ron Harvey May 25, 2008	Window Rock, Arizona	Enemy Way Ceremony, Church of God Native leadership
Jeff Yellowowl November 2008	Telephone interview	Foursquare Native leadership, contextualization
Cheryl Bear-Barnetson November 20, 2008	Telephone interview	dance, Foursquare Native leadership, drum
Paul Risser November 25, 2008	Telephone interview	Foursquare Native leadership
Kyle Taylor February 17, 2009	Muskogee, Oklahoma	dance, smudging, contextualization, language
Dan Lundy March 29, 2009	Siletz, Oregon	drum, talking circles, Foursquare Native leadership, contextualization

APPENDIX E

THE CHEROKEE STOMP DANCE, A HISTORICAL CASE STUDY

Here, I examine a dance that has been and is being integrated into Cherokee life as they follow Jesus: the Cherokee Stomp Dance. The Cherokee, due to Removal, call both the Southeastern and Southern Plains cultural areas home. I have already mentioned that Evan Jones allowed the Stomp Dance to be performed on church property as early as the 19th century. What complicates this issue are the differences between Euro-Americans and Natives in their approach to dance. For white Euro-Americans, dance has been historically artistic, sometimes spiritual or religious, but more widely recreational. For Native Americans, dance is prayer and a part of the renewal of creation, but not necessarily religious.[1] In the light of this difference it is easy to understand how the early missionaries to Natives, and especially the later American Holiness Movement, could have done damage to a culture by requiring an abstinence from dancing based upon a white man's experience.

The Stomp Dance is not exclusive to the Cherokee. Creeks and other tribes have practiced it as well. The dance is performed around a fire to the beat of a water drum that is small enough to be held in one hand. The remainder of the percussion emanates from the 'shackles' (rattles made of turtle shells or condensed milk tins sewn onto the top of cowboy boots or pieces of leather and worn on women's legs). The men sing in 'call and response'.

---

[1] Kidwell, Noley, and Tinker, *Native American Theology*, p. 12.

There is often a speech describing the history of the dance and the grounds on which it is played. Soon there is a meal. The dance then commences counter-clockwise. The leader and the men turn their faces and hands toward the fire, honoring it. There are many songs designated only for Stomp Dances. The people dance all night. Those who 'belong to the stomp grounds' sit under seven brush arbors. The others ring around that huge circle. There might also be a game of stickball.[2]

This dance will not be seen at a powwow, due to the fact that this dance has not been widely shared with other people. In 1889, many traditional Cherokees resisted the loss of tradition in Cherokee society and consequently revived the Keetoowah Society. A Cherokee named 'Redbird' Smith instituted the 'Nighthawk Keetoowah'. This group not only served to preserve old traditional practices but also opposed allotment of Cherokee tribal lands. The Keetoowah Society keeps the Stomp Grounds because they keep the Sacred Fire. They aid the memory of the people. Stomp Dances continue today in Oklahoma and North Carolina.[3]

Today, among the Eastern Cherokee in North Carolina, Walker Calhoun holds the Sacred Fire having brought it from Oklahoma. The following is included in a website for a recent PBS documentary entitled 'Indian Country Diaries':

> Anthropologists have recognized the power of oral history for at least the last 150 years. In 1887, a young Irish ethnologist, James Mooney, began writing down many of the Cherokee stories, songs and medicinal plant formulas. Oral history became part of the 'official' ... that is, written ... historical record. Mooney talked with the elders of the time – men like Ross Swimmer, Ayasta, Suyeta, John Ax, William Holland Thomas and Will West Long.
>
> Today, Will West Long's nephew Walker Calhoun is one of most respected and recognized authorities on Cherokee songs and oral history. Walker is featured in Spiral of Fire.

---

[2] McLoughlin, *Cherokees and Missionaries, 1789-1839*, pp. 207-08.
[3] Green and Fernandez, *The British Museum Encyclopedia of Native North America*, pp. 152-53.

Walker grew up speaking only Cherokee in the Big Cove community on the Qualla Boundary, where he still lives. There was not much money in his household, but his uncle was a respected medicine man, singer and storyteller. Walker learned the ancient songs and stories from Will West Long, who had learned from Swimmer, who had learned from his elders. By the time he was nine, Walker Calhoun knew all of the songs his uncle taught him.

When Walker was 12, he went to boarding school in Cherokee, North Carolina, and learned English. He served in the military during World War II in Europe.

In 1947, Will West Long passed away, and Walker began to pass on the traditions he had learned to his children and other students. He formed the Raven Rock Dancers with other members of his family. In 1988 – during celebrations marking the 150th anniversary of the Trail of Tears – Walker was honored at a gathering of the Eastern and Western Bands of the Cherokee and was asked to bring the sacred fire back from the Oklahoma Western Band to North Carolina.

He has received many awards including the National Folk Heritage Award from the National Endowment for the Arts in 1992. He also served as a consultant for the new National Museum of the American Indian in Washington, DC.[4]

The Cherokee Stomp dance, as suggested above, serves more than a social function. It has served the Cherokee and other tribes as a link to their history, functioning as what Pentecostals and other Christian groups might refer to as 'testimony'. Significant for the Removal Era, and probably the underlying function that caused Jones to allow it in the 1830s, is its statement of resistance or protest and confidential nature. One Cherokee legend, 'The Rabbit Escapes from the Wolves', connected with the Stomp Dance, bears reciting:

Some Wolves once caught the Rabbit and were going to eat him when he asked leave to show them a new dance he was practic-

---

[4] Frank Blythe and Carol Cornsilk, *Spiral of Fire*, PBS, (accessed June 16 2008); available from http://www.pbs.org/indiancountry/about. Walker is one of the few living links to the ancient oral history of the Cherokee.

ing. They knew that the Rabbit was a great song leader, and they wanted to learn the latest dance, so they agreed and made a ring about him while he got ready.

He patted his feet and began to dance around in a circle, singing:

Tlâge'sitûñ' gäli'sgi'sidâ'hä Ha'nia lîl lîl! Ha'nia lîl lîl! On the edge of the field I dance about Ha'nia lîl lîl! Ha'nia lîl lîl!

'Now', said the Rabbit, 'when I sing on the edge of the field, I dance that way' – and he danced over in that direction – 'and when I sing *lîl lîl!* you must all stamp your feet hard'.

The Wolves thought it fine. He began another round singing the same song, and danced a little nearer to the field, while the Wolves all stamped their feet. He sang louder and louder and danced nearer and nearer to the field until at the fourth song, when the Wolves were stamping as hard as they could and thinking only of the song, he made one jump and was off through the long grass.

They were after him at once, but he ran for a hollow stump and climbed up on the inside. When the Wolves got there one of them put his head inside to look up, but the Rabbit spit into his eye, so that he had to pull his head out again.

The others were afraid to try, and they went away, with the Rabbit still in the stump.[5]

It is not difficult to imagine the meaning this held for victims of government oppression. In the legend, the Cherokee could envision an escape from repression and ultimately from removal from their tribal lands. The eventual recovery of the Dance in the late 1880s coincides with the Ghost Dance movement that was amazingly universally widespread among American Indians and culminated in the Wounded Knee Massacre. The Cherokee Ghost Dance is not widely recognized, but represented a revitalization movement and a protest movement among the Cherokee.

---

[5] Mooney, *Myths of the Cherokee: Nineteenth Annual Report of the Bureau of American Ethnology to the Secretary of the Smithsonian Institution 1897-1898 by J.W. Powell Director, in Two Parts*, p. 274.

Data

Randy Woodley's first participation in a Stomp Dance (which Woodley refers to as, 'Our Native Cherokee dance') was in Oklahoma. '... [T]here was a deep sense in my soul that I had heard that music many times before. I was soaking all this in and feeling very fulfilled during this time among my own people'.[6] Another time while in Keetoowah dancing (possibly something akin to the Stomp Dance which is tied to this location), Woodley elaborates on his experience:

> As I reverently approached the mound, a strong sense of destiny filled my being. Suddenly I was pulled into a trance-like state. I began to sing, then dance – the entire time oblivious to where the rest of the group was standing. After about fifteen minutes of communing with God, I was exhausted and fell to the ground. I could only lie there and thank God for whatever He was doing. God – 'Yowah' met me there that day, the same God who visited my ancestors thousands of years prior. The same God who I had known for much of my life. The same God who sent His Son into the world for the Cherokees and for all people.[7]

Here we have a contextual Cherokee minister participating in the Stomp Dance and we are given a glimpse into the type of experience that such a minister has while dancing. The manifestations are highly Pentecostal or Charismatic in that they include trance, falling down and uses communion language that Pentecostals prefer when describing an experience in the Presence of God. Woodley's experience is fully contextualized in that he realizes continuity between the Christian heritage of his childhood and his affirmed Native identity in the ceremony.

Critical Contextualization

Again, the reader can see that the phenomenological examination, which Hiebert's model calls, for is done internally here by the Natives themselves. Randy Woodley's experience in this historic case

---

[6] Woodley, *Living in Color*, pp. 94-95.
[7] Woodley, *Living in Color*, pp. 134-35.

reveals how he, as a Native person, was transformed in the Stomp Dance to get more in touch with himself and his God. The practice of Stomp Dances on Baptist church grounds from the early Removal Period until now demonstrates how churches have not believed that performing the Stomp Dance has in any way compromised their commitment to Christ and his cross. The historic practice of performing the Stomp Dance is an example of Native Americans exercising spiritual discernment while evaluating old beliefs and practices in the light of biblical truth.

Examining further from another perspective, the missiologist Charles Kraft assists us as he recognizes that for past generations of Christian believers, any type of dance would have been held in suspicion and condemned in Native contexts (African, in his case), regardless of whether or not it resembled the dancing of the missionary's culture of origin. He describes the Africans, who danced in a circle around a drum. The missionaries condemned the practice, especially in the light of the 'empowerment and meaning issues' that were attached to the dance. The fear, according to Kraft, that prompted missionaries to exercise such censure, was 'fear of syncretism'.[8] Kraft goes on to describe two consequences of this type of censure due to fear of syncretism. The first is that the missionary unwittingly projects that the native culture is worthless, and second, he/she pushes the people into another, equally dangerous form of syncretism: the driving underground of native practices. This is what happened in the Removal Era for the Cherokees, with the exception of Evan Jones. Hiebert has also elaborated on this damage unwittingly done by missionaries, by describing the twofold detriment: it elevated Western culture as being Christian and also failed to provide a replacement practice.[9]

The discussion that Kraft gives concerning dance among Nigerians may not be completely applicable due to the less sexually suggestive movements in Native American dance (with the exception of dances like the Booger Dance, which are highly sexually suggestive).[10] Nevertheless, Kraft recognizes dance as serving as a 'vehicle

---

[8] Kraft, *Anthropology for Christian Witness*, pp. 259-60.

[9] Hiebert, Shaw, and Tienou, *Understanding Folk Religion*, p. 20.

[10] Laurence French and Jim Hornbuckle, *The Cherokee Perspective: Written by Eastern Cherokees* (Boone, NC: The Appalachian Consortium Press, 1981), pp. 126-28.

of enculturation' and as having the ability to communicate the values of a society. This function is observed in Woodley's experience as he encounters his Native roots in Keetoowah.[11]

Further engaging Kraft, in a positive way, I would agree that any rite, if the power of Satan is broken, can be used for God's service. Kraft's concerns about the meanings which lie behind any dance or practice do not particularly raise a problem with the Stomp Dance, due to the fact that the legendary background and essential meaning that the dance holds for the community was always redemptive. By this I mean that the significance of the dance, according to Green is the expression of the tribe's collective memory, the cohesiveness of the people's culture and the protest of the encroaching enemies to the tribe's land and future.[12] I feel, however, that Kraft stops short in his prescription for the avoidance of syncretism by limiting it to three resources: (1) our own interpretations and worldview; (2) biblical authors' writings and worldview; and (3) receptors' understandings and worldview.

Biblical Literature

Pentecostals would add another resource: the discernment of the Spirit as it relates to dance. John Wesley's Quadrilateral also seems to incorporate four sources for discernment: reason (our own), Scripture (biblical authors), tradition (receptors worldview), and experience (the witness of the Spirit). Acts 15 describes the process, concluding:

> It seemed good to the Holy Spirit and to us not to burden you with anything beyond the following requirements: You are to abstain from food sacrificed to idols, from blood, from the meat of strangled animals and from sexual immorality. You will do well to avoid these things (Acts 15.28-29).

Though this passage is often used to describe the process of contextualization, which often includes searching the Scriptures, this text does not mention Bible study (though the chapter does), but does mention 'it seemed good to the Holy Spirit and to us'. This Pentecostal 'Discerning the Spirit(s)' is developing into an entire

---

[11] Kraft, *Anthropology for Christian Witness*, pp. 265-66.
[12] Kraft, *Anthropology for Christian Witness*, p. 213.

Theology of Religions through the work of scholars like Amos Yong and Tony Richie.[13]

Woodley cites what he calls Hiebert's four steps to critical contextualization. Hiebert advocates that participant observers look at the culture in as objective a way as possible, without judging it; then test the truth claims of the culture in light of the Scriptures and the culture; then evaluate the response to the existing beliefs in light of their new biblical understanding, using the community as a judge; and then finally accept, reject, or reformulate the cultural practice to give it Christian meaning.[14]

Hiebert provides this four-step model of critical contextualization into which Native American experiences can be applied. In the model, folk religions answer the middle ground of issues that pertain to everyday life. It is my opinion that for tribes like the Cherokee, dealing with the folk religious middle is not enough. They have creation stories and myths of origin that have bearing on their everyday practice. The responsible missiologist will have to engage such stories and myths that probably overlap higher and lower religious concerns. Woodley has effectively pointed out that talking opossums and birds in Cherokee myth are not much different from a talking donkey in Scripture.[15] If we say that Cherokee tradition is a folk religion and not a religion 'in the Western sense', it further underlines the need for a postmodern revision of what religions really are. Is a religion a worldview that merely promises future transcendence or that which immanently transforms and influences the lives of God's people?

The Ghost Dance Movement with its Millenarian concern, eschatological resurrection, and earth renewal reveals the important interplay between the high and middle worlds for Native peoples. It is a dance (folk practice to some, worship in King David's context of 2 Sam. 6.20-23) that is connected to an apocalyptic event. In this we see the middle and the high religion interacting integratively. The model constructed for us by Hiebert is extremely helpful to move us from the anthropological emphasis of what Kraft describes, but may not fully provide a way to evaluate the spiritual experiences that Woodley is describing as a contextual Indian.

---

[13] Yong, *Discerning the Spirit(s)*; and Richie, *Speaking by the Spirit*.
[14] Hiebert, Shaw, and Tienou, *Understanding Folk Religion*, p. 22.
[15] Woodley, *Living in Color*, p. 50.

I want to reiterate that neither Kraft nor Hiebert include in their steps the important dimension of the discernment of the Spirit. Woodley also makes an important point when he emphasizes that it is important not only 'how' we approach the task of critical contextualization, but also 'who takes part in the process'.[16] The history of Native American missions demands that Euro-Americans step aside and allow Natives to do the constructing, leave the Euro-Americans to the business of encouraging and equipping.

Woodley is such a constructionist. He writes: 'Contextualization could simply mean to present the good news of the kingdom of Jesus Christ in a way that people can understand in their own context-but it is a much deeper process'.[17] We should not be surprised to be reminded that the Stomp Dance, an 'expressive aspect of culture' deals with the affective nature of spiritual experience, as Woodley's own experience shows.

What missiologists have tended to emphasize is the analogical function that rituals like dance can serve. How are we to understand this 'much deeper process'? It may be helpful for us to be reminded that in the Native American cultural context, 'Native Christians consider personal and collective experience to play a central role in the development of spiritual insight'.[18] Woodley says on one occasion, which he prefaces with a Native translation of Heb. 1.1-3:

> Long ago Creator spoke many times and in many ways to our ancestors through the prophets. But now in these final days, He has spoken to us through his Son. Creator promised everything to the Son as an inheritance, and through the Son he made the universe and everything in it. The Son reflects Creator's own glory, and everything about him represents Creator exactly. He sustains the universe by the mighty power of his command. I like this last one because it connects us to our ancestors. All the promises He made to them are fulfilled in Jesus. He is the One who created the world. He created the water where we go pray

---

[16] Woodley, *When Going to Church Is Sin and Other Essays on Native American Christian Missions*, p. 144.

[17] Woodley, *When Going to Church Is Sin and Other Essays on Native American Christian Missions*, p. 140.

[18] James Treat, *Native and Christian: Indigenous Voices on Religious Identity in the United States and Canada* (New York: Routledge, 1996), p. 13.

in the mornings. He created the fire where we dance and sing. He created the turtles where we get our rattles. He created the smoke that raises up to honor Him. To me it says that any ceremony that is from the Great Spirit will point to Him. If it is true, then it will point to the Truth. Everything that is true will point to Him. He is the fulfillment of the sacred fire, the cleansing fire, the water ceremonies, the sweat lodge and all other things. They all point to Him ... When I pray at water I know He is the One I am thanking. When I dance, I dance to Him. When I bless myself with the cedar fire I am realizing that it is His blood that cleanses me. And when I sweat in the O'si I am thanking Him for a cleansing that never ends.[19]

Much of what Woodley is saying here clearly refers to his experience in the Stomp Dance. He understands the ceremonies to be a gift from the Creator, the Father of our Lord Jesus Christ, and that these ceremonies all point to Jesus. This is a critical contextualization of dances, like the Stomp Dance, and a truly contextualized understanding.

Transformed Praxis

The act of coming to a contextualized understanding of dances, like the Cherokee Stomp Dance, is not a new exercise. In the emerging Native American Theological debate, the dance has frequently been considered. It is placed within the category of earth renewal ceremonies.[20] Here I acknowledge that Native Americans, if welcomed into the theological discussion, hold a future for the post-modern Church that could eventually help God's people to save the earth rather than destroy it through a weak stewardship approach to ecology.

Thus, dances like the Stomp Dance and also the Green Corn Dance carry eschatological and ecological significance. Imagine seasonal, even Earth Day celebrations, where a fully contextualized Native American dance could be understood as a sacrament for the Church as believers pray and work for the renewal of the earth's

---

[19] Woodley, *When Going to Church Is Sin and Other Essays on Native American Christian Missions*, pp. 27-28.

[20] Kidwell, Noley, and Tinker, *Native American Theology*, p. 12.

life. This represents one of the many hopes that Native Christians hold for the future of the Church worldwide.

Toward a Contextual Sacramental Theology of the Stomp Dance

If we approach the Last Supper narrative, as Christians have for centuries, we will see the significance that it has held theologically for believers. In Mk 14.22-25 we read,

> While they were eating, Jesus took bread, gave thanks and broke it, and gave it to his disciples, saying, 'Take it; this is my body'. Then he took the cup, gave thanks and offered it to them, and they all drank from it. 'This is my blood of the covenant, which is poured out for many', he said to them. 'I tell you the truth, I will not drink again of the fruit of the vine until that day when I drink it anew in the kingdom of God'.

The Synoptic texts have been utilized in Christian worship as believers have observed the Lord's Supper or Communion since the day the Lord Jesus Christ first instituted it. In this respect, John Wesley would have labeled it an 'Instituted Means of Grace'. Shaw uses the Lord's Supper as an example of contextualization.

> The occasion and means of celebrating the 'Lord's supper' provides a case in point. Should this be regularly incorporated into the worship service or be a separate celebration in believers' homes? How should the 'elements' be represented – by local materials such as coconut meat and milk or possible imported items like grape juice (or even wine) and bread? To answer these questions, Christians need to appreciate the concepts and symbolic meanings process. Such a recognition of the relationship between a particular context, Scripture and the church enables the theology that develops to serve the plan for people in all times and places.[21]

This is helpful for the purposes of this study because it recognizes precedence for using the Lord's Supper as a sample case for contextualization. One need only reflect on the varieties of expres-

---

[21] R.D. Shaw, 'Contextualizing the Power and the Glory', *International Journal of Frontier Missions* 12.3 (1995), p. 158.

sions of this sacrament or ordinance just in North American churches to realize the possibilities for plurality in worship.

Within the Last Supper, Pentecostal theology has seen, in the words of R. Hollis Gause, 'rapture, rapport and proleptic'.[22] Gause calls this a 'Theology of Worship'. What this means simply is that the Lord's Supper enables the Church to reflect upon three realities: (1) The rapture of spiritual graces in the individual experience as the worshiper reflects upon the Passion event in 'this is my body'; (2) the rapport within the communal aspect of collective worshipers as part of a larger community of mutual fellowship in that 'they all drank from it'; and (3) the prophetic anticipation of the future restitution of all things in that he will 'drink it anew in the kingdom of God'.

In a similar way the Stomp Dance holds significance for at least the Creek and Cherokee tribes. It was a secretive ceremony that was celebrated historically during a time of persecution. The legend upon which it is related speaks of a rabbit that is prisoner to a pack of wolves. He victoriously tricks his enemies through a dance in which he slips away into 'another world'. The Stomp Dancers view the dance as a renewal of the earth and was historically revived during a time of national loss and grief. Though the Stomp Dance is not a biblically instituted means of grace, yet a contextualized sacrament could be developing as Natives, like Randy Woodley, revision the practice.

---

[22] Kimberly E. Alexander and R.H. Gause, *Women in Leadership: A Pentecostal Perspective* (Cleveland, TN: The Center For Pentecostal Leadership and Care, 2006), p. 198.

BIBLIOGRAPHY

Alexander, Corky, "The Evangelistic Legacy of the Klaudt Indian Family",
  Church of God Evangel 100.6 (June 2010), p. 17.
Alexander, Kimberly E., and R.H. Gause, *Women in Leadership: A Pentecostal
  Perspective* (Cleveland, TN: The Center For Pentecostal Leadership and Care,
  2006).
Alexander, Kimberly Ervin, *Pentecostal Healing: Models in Theology and Practice*
  (JPTSup, 29; Blandford Forum, UK: Deo Publishing, 2006).
Allen, Roland, *The Spontaneous Expansion of the Church and the Causes Which Hinder It*
  (Grand Rapids: Eerdmans, 1962).
Barnetson, Randy, 'Telephone Interview with Randy Barnetson' Santa Fe
  Springs, CA (2007).
Bear-Barnetson, Cheryl, 'Introduction to First Nations Ministry: Everything One
  Wants to Know, but Is Afraid They Are Too White to Ask', Professional
  Ministry Research Project, The King's Seminary, 2009.
 – 'Cheryl Bear-Barnetson Interview' Vancouver, BC (2008).
Berkhofer, R.F., *Salvation and the Savage: An Analysis of Protestant Missions and
  American Indian Response, 1787-1862* (Lexington: University of Kentucky Press,
  1965).
Bevans, Stephen, *Models of Contextual Theology* (Maryknoll: Orbis Books, 1992).
Blythe, Frank, and Carol Cornsilk, *Spiral of Fire*, PBS (accessed June 16 2008;
  Available from http://www.pbs.org/indiancountry/about).
Boas, F., and R. Benedict, *General Anthropology* (Boston: Pub. for the US Armed
  forces institute by Heath, 1944).
Bosch, David J., *Transforming Mission: Paradigm Shifts in Theology of Mission*
  (Maryknoll, NY: Orbis Books, 1991).
Brafman, O., and R.A. Beckstrom, *The Starfish and the Spider: The Unstoppable Power
  of Leaderless Organizations* (New York: Portfolio, 2006).
Brown, Joseph Epes, *The Sacred Pipe: Black Elk's Account of the Seven Rites of the
  Oglala Sioux* (Civilization of the American Indian Series: Norman, OK:
  University of Oklahoma Press, 1989).
Brown, Larry 'Grizz', 'Telephone Interview with Larry "Grizz" Brown' Apple
  Valley, CA (2007).
Burgess, S.M., and E.M. Van der Maas (eds.), *The New International Dictionary of
  Pentecostal and Charismatic Movements* (Grand Rapids: Zondervan Pub. House,
  2002).
Conn, Charles W., *Like a Mighty Army: A History of the Church of God* (Cleveland:
  Pathway Press, 1977).

– *Like a Mighty Army: A History of the Church of God Definitive Edition* (Cleveland: Pathway Press, 1994).

Cox, H., *Fire from Heaven: The Rise of Pentecostal Spirituality and the Reshaping of Religion in the Twenty-First Century* (Reading, MA: Addison Wesley Publishing Company, 1994).

Deloria, Vine, Jr., (Standing Rock Sioux), *God Is Red: A Native View of Religion* (Golden: North American Press, Second edn, 1973).

– *Custer Died for Your Sins: An Indian Manifesto* (Norman: University of Oklahoma Press, 1989/1969).

Dennison, Johnson, 'Spiritual Perspectives: The Navajo Enemy Way Ceremony', *Gallup Independent* (Web Edition) June 25, 2005.

Dorsey, G.A., and J.R. Murie, *Notes on Skidi Pawnee Society* (Whitefish, MT: Kessinger Publishing, 2006).

Dugan, K.M., *The Vision Quest of the Plains Indians: Its Spiritual Significance* (Lewiston, NY: Edwin Mellen Press, 1985).

Edmunds, R.D., *American Indian Leaders: Studies in Diversity* (Lincoln, NE: University of Nebraska Press, 1980).

Erickson, P.A., and L.D. Murphy, *A History of Anthropological Theory* (Peterborough, ON: Broadview Press, 2003).

Feather, F.D., and R. Robinson, *Exploring Native American Wisdom: Lore, Traditions, and Rituals That Connect Us All* (Franklin Lakes, NJ: Career Press, 2003).

Finzel, H., *Top Ten Mistakes Leaders Make* (Colorado Springs, CO: Cook Communications Ministries International, 2000).

Finzel, Hans, *Change Is Like a Slinky* (Northfield, VT: Northfield Publishing, 2004).

Fletcher, A.C., J.R. Murie, and E.S. Tracy, *The Hako: A Pawnee Ceremony* (Washington, DC: Govt. Print. Off., 1904).

French, Laurence, and Jim Hornbuckle, *The Cherokee Perspective: Written by Eastern Cherokees* (Boone, NC: The Appalachian Consortium Press, 1981).

Gefen, Gavriel, 'Re-Contextualization: Restoring the Biblical Message to a Jewish Israeli Context', *Journal of North American Institute for Indigenous Theological Studies* 4 (2006), pp. 5-28.

Tom Claus and Dale W. Kietzman (eds.), *Christian Leadership in Indian America* (Chicago: Moody Press, 1976), p. 122.

Green, Rayna, and Melanie Fernandez, *The British Museum Encyclopedia of Native North America* (Bloomington, IN: Indiana University Press, 1999).

Harvey, Ron, 'Window Rock Church of God Interview', Window Rock (2008).

Hayward, Douglas, 'Foundations for Critical Contextualization: Preliminary Considerations for Doing Contextualization among First Nations Christians', *Journal of North American Institute for Indigenous Theological Studies* 1.1 (2003), pp. 37-52.

Hiebert, Paul G., *Cultural Anthropology* (Grand Rapids: Baker Book House, Second edn, 1983).

– *Anthropological Insights for Missionaries* (Grand Rapids: Baker Book House, 1985).

– *Anthropological Reflections on Missiological Issues* (Grand Rapids: Baker Book House, 1994).

Hiebert, Paul G., and Frances F. Hiebert, *Case Studies in Missions* (Grand Rapids, MI: Baker Book House, 1987).

Hiebert, Paul G., R. Daniel Shaw, and Tite Tiénou, *Understanding Folk Religion: A Christian Response to Popular Beliefs and Practices* (Grand Rapids: Baker Book House, 1999).

Hiebert, P.G., 'The Flaw of the Excluded Middle', *Missiology: An International Review* 10.1 (1982), pp. 35-47.

Hollenweger, W.J., *The Pentecostals* (London: SCM, 1972).

– *Pentecostalism: Origins and Developments Worldwide* (Peabody, MA: Hendrickson Publishers, 1997).

Howard, J.H., 'Pan-Indian Culture of Oklahoma', *The Scientific Monthly* 81.5 (1955), pp. 215-20.

Jacobs, Adrian, *Aboriginal Christianity: The Way It Was Meant to Be* (Rapid City, SD: Adrian Jacobs, 1998).

Jacobs, Adrian, Richard Twiss, and Terry Leblanc, 'Culture, Christian Faith and Error', *The Journal of the North American Institute for Indigenous Theological Studies* 1.1 (2003), pp. 5-36.

Jones, E. Stanley, *The Christ of the Indian Road* (New York: Abingdon press, 1925).

Josephy, A.M., *500 Nations: An Illustrated History of North American Indians* (New York: Alfred A. Knopf, 1994).

Josephy, A.M., *The Indian Heritage of America* (Wilmington, MA: Mariner Books, 1991).

Kärkkäinen, V.M., *An Introduction to the Theology of Religions: Biblical, Historical and Contemporary Perspectives* (Downers Grove: InterVarsity Press, 2003).

Kidwell, C.S., *Choctaws and Missionaries in Mississippi, 1818-1918* (Norman: University of Oklahoma Press, 1995).

Kidwell, C.S., H. Noley, and G.E. Tinker, *Native American Theology* (Maryknoll, NY: Orbis Books, 2001).

King, M.L., *Strength to Love* (Minneapolis, MN: Fortress Press, 1982).

Kittel, G., and G. Friedrich, *The Theological Dictionary of the New Testament Abridged in One Volume*, (Grand Rapids, MI: Eerdmans, 1985).

Kraft, C.H., *Christianity in Culture* (Maryknoll, NY: Orbis Books, 1984).

Kraft, Charles H., *Anthropology for Christian Witness* (Maryknoll: Orbis, 1996).

Kroeber, A.L., *Cultural and Natural Areas of Native North America* (Berkeley, CA: University of California Press, 1963).

– *Handbook of the Indians of California* (Mineola, NY: Dover Pub., 1976).

Land, Steven, *Pentecostal Spirituality* (JPTSup, 1; Sheffield: Sheffield Academic Press, 1993).

Lingenfelter, Sherwood, *Agents of Transformation: A Guide for Effective Cross-Cultural Ministry* (Grand Rapids: Baker Book House, 1996).

– *Transforming Culture: A Challenge for Christian Mission* (Grand Rapids: Baker Book House, 1998).

Linton, R., *The Sacrifice to the Morning Star by the Skidi Pawnee* (Chicago, IL: Field Museum of Natural History, 1922).

– *The Thunder Ceremony of the Pawnee* (Chicago, IL: Field Museum of Natural History, 1922).

– *Annual Ceremony of the Pawnee Medicine Men* (Chicago, IL: Field Museum of Natural History,1923).

– *Use of Tobacco among North American Indians* (Chicago, IL: Field Museum of Natural History, 1924).

Linton, Ralph, *Acculturation in Seven American Indian Tribes* (Gloucester: Peter Smith, 1963).

Lundy, Dan, 'Interview', Siletz (2009).

Lyon, W.S., *Encyclopedia of Native American Healing* (New York: WW Norton & Company, 1998).

Malinowski, B., *Argonauts of the Western Pacific* (Prospect, IL: Malinowski Press, 2008).

McDonald, Mark, 'The Gospel Comes to North America', *Journal of North American Institute for Indigenous Theological Studies* 4 (2006), pp. 129-38.

McLoughlin, W.G., *Cherokees and Missionaries, 1789-1839* (Norman: University of Oklahoma Press, 1995).

Mooney, James, *Myths of the Cherokee: Nineteenth Annual Report of the Bureau of American Ethnology to the Secretary of the Smithsonian Institution 1897-1898 by J.W. Powell Director, in Two Parts* (St. Clair Shores: Scholarly Press, 1970 /1990).

Murie, J.R., *Pawnee Indian Societies* (New York: The Trustees, 1914).

Murie, J.R., and D.R. Parks, *Ceremonies of the Pawnee* (Washington, DC: Smithsonian Institution Press, 1981).

Neihardt, J.G., *Black Elk Speaks* (Lincoln, NE: Bison Books, 2004).

Neihardt, John, *When the Tree Flowered: The Story of Eagle Voice, a Sioux Indian* (Lincoln, NE: University of Nebraska Press, new edn, 1991).

Operation Compassion Partners with Montana Missionary (Cleveland, TN: Operation Compassion, 2004).

Owusu, H., *Symbols of Native America* (New York: Sterling Pub. Co., 1999).

Pinnock, C.H., *Flame of Love: A Theology of the Holy Spirit* (Downers Grove: InterVarsity Press, 1999).

Porterfield, A., *Healing in the History of Christianity* (New York: Oxford University Press, 2005).

Powers, William K., *Oglala Religion* (Lincoln: University of Nebraska Press, 1977).

– *Yuwipi: Vision and Experience in Oglala Ritual* (Lincoln: University of Nebraska Press, 1982).

– *Beyond the Vision: Essays on American Indian Culture* (Norman, OK: University of Oklahoma Press, 1987).

– *Wardance: Plains Indian Musical Performance* (Tuscon, AZ: The University of Arizona Press, 1990).

– 'Native American Music of the Twentieth Century', in Robert Santelli, Holly George-Warren, and Jim Brown (eds.), *American Roots Music* (New York: Harry N. Abrams, 2001), pp. 144-59.

Richie, Tony L., 'God's Fairness to People of All Faiths: A Respectful Proposal to Pentecostals for Discussion Regarding World Religions', *Pneuma* 28.1 (2006), pp. 105-19.

– 'Revamping Pentecostal Evangelism: Appropriating Walter J. Hollenweger's Radical Proposal', *International Review of Mission* 96.382-383 (2007), pp. 343-54.

– 'Approaching the Problem of Religious Truth in a Pluralistic World: A Pentecostal-Charismatic Contribution', *Journal of Ecumenical Studies* 43.3 (2008), pp. 351-69.

– *Speaking by the Spirit: A Pentecostal Model for Interreligious Dialogue* (Lexington, KY: Emeth Press, 2011).

Richardson, D., *Eternity in Their Hearts* (Ventura, CA: Regal books, 1984).

– *Peace Child* (Ventura, CA: Regal Books, 1974).

Risser, Paul, 'Telephone Interview with Dr. Paul Risser' (2008).

Robeck, Cecil M., Jr., *The Azusa Street Mission and Revival: The Birth of the Global Pentecostal Movement* (Nashville: Thomas Nelson, 2006).

Rodgers, D.J., *Northern Harvest: Pentecostalism in North Dakota* (Bismarck: North Dakota District Council of the Assemblies of God, 2003).

Saggio, J.J., and Jim Dempsey, *American Indian College: A Witness to the Tribes* (Springfield: Gospel Publishing House, 2008).

Shaw, R.D., 'A Samo Theology of Mediumship: A Case Study of Local Theologizing and Global Reflection', in Carole M. Cusack and Christopher H. Hartney (eds.), *The International Festschrift for Garry W. Trompf* (Leiden: Brill, 2009).

– 'Contextualization' (Personal email communication, May 1, 2009).

– 'Contextualizing the Power and the Glory', *International Journal of Frontier Missions* 12.3 (1995), p. 6.

– 'Of Grass, Food, and Hospitality: The Role of Cognitive Studies in the Translation/Communication Task', *Scriptura* 96 (2007), pp. 501-22.

– *Transculturation: The Cultural Factor in Translation and Other Communication Tasks* (Pasadena: William Carey Library, 1988).

Shaw, R.D., and C.E. Van Engen, *Communicating God's Word in a Complex World: God's Truth or Hocus Pocus?* (Lanham, MD: Rowman & Littlefield, 2003).

Smith, Craig S., *Boundary Lines: The Issue of Christ, Indigenous Worship and Native American Culture* (Prince Albert, Sask.: N.C.E.M, 2001).

Stolzman, William, *The Pipe and Christ: A Christian-Sioux Dialogue* (Chamberlin: Tipi Press, 6th edn, 1998).

Tarango, Angela, '"Choosing the Jesus Way:" the Assemblies of God's Home Missions to American Indians and the Development of a Pentecostal Indian Identity' (PhD diss., Duke University, 2009).

Taylor, J.V., *The Primal Vision: Christian Presence Amid African Religion* (Minneapolis, MN: Fortress Press, 1963).

Taylor, Kyle, 'Personal Interview', Muskogee, OK (2009).

Thomas, John Christopher, *Footwashing in the Gospel of John and the Johannine Community* (JSNTSup, 61; Sheffield: JSOT Press, 1991).

– *The Spirit of the New Testament* (Blandford Forum, UK: Deo, 2005).

Thorsen, D.A.D., *Wesleyan Quadrilateral: Scripture, Tradition, Reason & Experience as a Model of Evangelical Theology* (Grand Rapids, MI: Zondervan, 1990).

Tom, Jerry, and Ron Harvey, 'Window Rock Church of God Interview', Window Rock (2008).

Treat, James, *Native and Christian: Indigenous Voices on Religious Identity in the United States and Canada* (New York: Routledge, 1996).

Turner, V.W., *The Forest of Symbols: Aspects of Ndembu Ritual* (Ithaca, NY: Cornell University Press, 1967).

Twiss, Richard, *Dancing Our Prayers: Perspectives on Syncretism, Critical Contextualization and Cultural Practices in First Nations Ministry* (Vancouver: Wiconi Press, 2002).

– *One Church Many Tribes: Following Jesus the Way God Made You* (Ventura: Regal, 2000).

Waldrop, Richard, 'Salvation History and the Mission of God: Implications for the Mission of the Church among Native Americans', Paper presented at The Missiology of Jamestown Consultation, Regent University, Virginia Beach, Virginia, May 28-29, 2008.

Walker, Paul H., *Paths of a Pioneer* (Cleveland, TN: Pathway Press, 1970).

Wallace, Anthony F.C., 'Revitalization Movements', *American Anthropologist* 58 (1956), pp. 264-81.

Wigram, Tony, Inge Nygaard Pedersen, and Lars Ole Bonde, *A Comprehensive Guide to Music Therapy: Theory, Clinical Practice, Research, and Training* (London: Jessica Kingsley Publishers, 2002).

Wilson, J., *The Earth Shall Weep: A History of Native America* (New York: Grove Press, 2000).

Woodley, Randy, *Living in Color: Embracing God's Passion for Ethnic Diversity* (Downers Grove: InterVarsity Press, 2001).

– *When Going to Church Is Sin and Other Essays on Native American Christian Missions* (Garden City: Morgan James, 2007).

Yong, A., *Discerning the Spirit(s): A Pentecostal-Charismatic Contribution to Christian Theology of Religions* (JPTSup, 20; Sheffield: Sheffield Academic Press, 2000).

INDEX OF BIBLICAL REFERENCES

GENERAL INDEX

www.ingramcontent.com/pod-product-compliance
Lightning Source LLC
Chambersburg PA
CBHW072347090426
42741CB00012B/2954